ST. VINCENT
FERRER

ANGEL OF THE JUDGMENT

St. Vincent Ferrer
"The Angel of the Judgment"
1350-1419

ST. VINCENT FERRER

ANGEL OF THE JUDGMENT

By

Fr. Andrew Pradel, O.P.

Translated from the French by
Fr. T. A. Dixon, O.P.

"And I saw another angel flying through the midst of heaven, having the eternal gospel, to preach unto them that sit upon the earth, and over every nation, and tribe, and tongue, and people: saying with a loud voice: Fear the Lord, and give him honour, because the hour of his judgment is come. . ."

—Apocalypse 14:6-7

TAN Books
Charlotte, North Carolina

Having at the request of the Very Reverend Father Provincial read the work entitled *St. Vincent Ferrer, of the Order of Friar Preachers: His Life, Spiritual Teaching, and Practical Devotion*, we have found nothing therein but what is conducive to the edification of the faithful.

— Fr. J. M. Monsabré, Ord. Praed.
Fr. T. Bourard, Ord. Praed., L.S.T.

Having seen the above approbation, we sanction the publication of the work entitled *St. Vincent Ferrer,* etc.

— Fr. A. N. Saudreau, Ord. Praed.
Provincial of the French Province

Imprimatur: A. de Pous
Vicar General, Toulouse
October 9, 1863

Nihil Obstat: Fr. Raymond Palmer, Ord. Praed.
Censor Deputatus

Imprimatur: ✛ Henry Edward
Cardinal Archbishop of Westminster

Published by R. Washbourne, London, in 1875 as *St. Vincent Ferrer, of the Order of Friar Preachers: His Life, Spiritual Teaching, and Practical Devotion*. The first of these three parts (his Life) was retypeset with minor editing of language and republished in 2000 by TAN Books with the addition of pictures.

ISBN: 978-0-89555-686-8

Library of Congress Control No.: 00-134505

Printed and bound in the United States of America.

TAN Books
Charlotte, North Carolina
www.TANBooks.com

2000

To his
Brethren and Sisters in St. Dominic,
Spread through England, Ireland and America,
This work rendered into English
Is affectionately dedicated by
The Translator.

St. Peter's Priory, Hinckley
Feast of St. Dominic
August 4, 1875

St. Vincent Ferrer as portrayed by an artist.

CONTENTS

—SECTION THREE—

THE MIRACULOUS APOSTOLATE
OF ST. VINCENT FERRER. 1398-1419.

—SECTION FOUR—

THE VIRTUES OF ST. VINCENT FERRER.

—SECTION FIVE—

THE MARVELOUS GIFTS WHICH SHONE FORTH IN ST. VINCENT FERRER.

Preface

A DESCRIPTION of the marvelous influence exercised by St. Vincent Ferrer on his age is not the principal design of the work which we offer to the public. In an admirable biography of this great man, the Abbé Bayle has traced out the most salient points in his character. Therefore, to reproduce in the following pages the picture which he has drawn would be foreign to our purpose. Our intention, then, is rather to initiate the pious public, and especially the Dominican family, into the intimate life and heroic virtues of the man of God, in order that they may imitate him, according to the degree of perfection to which each soul is divinely called. It would, indeed, be a strange illusion to imagine that there was much more to be admired than imitated in this remarkable life. We can, on the contrary, mold ourselves in many ways on this model, especially when it has reference to interior dispositions.

Father Teoli, a religious of our Order who lived in the last century and who wrote the most complete and accurate life of our Saint, has furnished us with the basis of our work. Following the example of this praiseworthy writer, we have not hesitated to relate certain traits well calculated to lead us to admire the stupendous and supreme power of working miracles which God sometimes accords to His Saints. It should be well borne in mind that the facts which we reveal rest on documents worthy of belief and respect, and that we address ourselves to pious readers. But this class admits the divine marvels the more readily in proportion as they who compose it are less carnal and more pure. We moreover willingly repeat, with Father Teoli, that in the facts here recorded, as well as in the title of Blessed which we have applied to certain personages whose veneration has not yet received the formal sanction of the Holy See, our intention is not to speak as though we had authority in the Church; we merely propose them with the guarantees of a purely human authority.

May our publication be serviceable to you, dear reader! Should it produce any good in you, be pleased, in return, to remember us in your prayers to the Saint whom we shall have venerated together. And you will crown this charity which we hope for from you if you will join to it a particular intention in favor of some pious persons who have afforded us useful and friendly help in the accomplishment of this work.

ST. VINCENT FERRER

FERRER

ANGEL OF THE JUDGMENT

—SECTION ONE—

FROM THE SAINT'S BIRTH
TO HIS RELIGIOUS PROFESSION.
1350-1368.

Chapter 1

Prodigies which Preceded the Birth of
St. Vincent Ferrer—Baptism, Infancy and
Childhood of St. Vincent.

IN the middle of the fourteenth century, there
dwelt at Valencia, in Spain, a pious couple who
were not less distinguished by birth than by the
virtues which adorned their lives. These were
William Ferrer, a descendant of an ancient Cat-
alonian family, and Constance Miguel, the daughter of a naval officer and kinswoman of the Bishop
of Valencia. They had already been blessed with
two children when a third was born to them on the
23rd of January, in the year 1350.

History affirms that certain remarkable signs
preceded the birth of this child of benediction.
One night while the father slept, he dreamed that
he entered the church of the Dominicans at Valencia when one of that Order was preaching to the
multitude from the pulpit and that the preacher,
turning toward him, addressed him in these words:
"I felicitate you, William. In a few days you will
have a son who will become a prodigy of learning

and sanctity. He will be the object of your delight and the honor of your house. The world will resound with the fame of his wondrous deeds; he will fill Heaven with joy and Hell with terror. He will put on the habit which I wear, and will be received in the Church with universal joy as one of its first Apostles." Then it seemed to him that the people, who had attentively listened to what was said, thanked God with a loud voice for the marvelous news and offered him their felicitations likewise. Delighted at these consoling predictions, he joined his thanksgiving to that of the multitude. When he awoke, he related to his spouse all that had transpired in the course of his dream, and they resolved to confer with their kinsman, the Bishop. To William's account of what had occurred, Constance added two things equally singular which she had herself experienced. The first was the fact that from the commencement of her pregnancy, she had felt none of the pains which usually accompany that state; and the second, that she frequently fancied she had heard the child, who was near its birth, give utterance to cries that resembled the barking of a little dog—a circumstance much resembling the vision of Blessed Jane of Aza, the mother of St. Dominic.

The prelate clearly understood the meaning of these mysterious signs and said to them: "Rejoice in the Lord; the child which you are about to bring into the world will be a worthy son of St. Dominic and will be called to do much good among the people by his preaching. Take great care of him and educate him holily, that he may correspond to the singular graces with which God will endow him."[1]

As if to confirm the high opinion which was conceived of this child, God was pleased to work, while it was still in the maternal womb, and by its mediation, a remarkable prodigy. Constance went one day to visit a blind woman on whom she was accustomed to bestow a monthly alms, and having given it to her as usual, she added, "My daughter, pray to God that the child which I bear may arrive safely." The blind woman bent her head to the mother's bosom and said, "May God bestow that favor on you!" At the same instant her material blindness left her, and being suddenly illuminated in her soul with prophetic light, she exclaimed, "Madam, it is an angel you have, and it is he who has cured me of my affliction." The child, like another John the Baptist, applauded the words of the poor woman by leaping in the womb; the mother herself gave testimony of it.[2]

Such were the signs that preceded the birth of Vincent Ferrer. This birth was an event for the whole city. The principal inhabitants made it a point of duty to accompany the newborn to the baptismal font. Besides a municipal deputation, three of the chief magistrates were present; and as they could not agree on the name that was to be given to this predestined child, the priest who administered the Sacrament was divinely inspired to name him *Vincent*, a name that was in every way adapted to his future destiny inasmuch as he would one day attack so vigorously, and conquer so gloriously, sin, the world, the flesh and the devil.

Constance was unwilling that her son should be committed to the care of a strange nurse. This child was too precious to allow anyone but herself to bestow on him the cares which tender infancy requires—cares which are doubtless wearisome, but nevertheless always sweet to a mother's heart. She was amply rewarded for this devotedness on her part, for the little Saint gave her but small trouble. Seldom did he cry, and he would remain tranquil wherever his mother placed him. When not asleep in his cradle, he was peaceful and almost recollected. His open eyes would search eagerly for his mother, without being moistened with tears. Nature exhausted her gifts on his behalf. To a charming disposition with which she endowed him, he joined also a countenance that was so sweet, well-shaped and sympathetic that all delighted to gaze upon him and to caress him.[3]

An extraordinary event contributed not a little to increase his renown in the city. Vincent was yet in his cradle and had hardly begun to lisp, when Valencia was desolated by a continued drought. Public prayers were offered up to obtain a refreshing rain, but not a cloud appeared in the sky. The whole population groaned under the calamity, and Constance shared the common affliction, when one day, expressing her uneasiness, she heard the child in swathing clothes distinctly pronounce these words: "If you wish for rain, carry me in procession, and you shall be favorably heard." Cheered as well as surprised at these miraculous words, Constance hastened to the city magistrates to impart to them her message. The latter, considering on the one hand the probity and good sense of the mother, and on the other hand the marvelous signs which had already drawn public attention to the child, decreed that the procession thus indicated should take place. The little Vincent was carried triumphantly, and scarcely had the procession ended when the sky became suddenly overcast, and copious rains fell for several hours upon the parched earth.[4] This and other miracles bore Vincent's name to the court of the King of Aragon. Queen Eleanor, coming to Valencia, caused him to be taken to her palace that she might see him and caress him.

In learning to speak, the child learned also how to pray and was instructed especially in the mysteries of faith. These instructions were imprinted on his soul as upon soft wax, but once they had taken root, they attained the solidity of bronze. There was no need to teach him twice the same lesson on religious matters. This sacred seed bore in his heart its salutary fruits. Penetrated with a sovereign fear of God and animated with a great desire for good, he carefully avoided everything that could, even in the smallest degree, tarnish his innocence.

From his fifth year, he showed an intelligence far above his age which inspired his companions and others with singular veneration for him. He began to study when only six years old, and his masters discovered in him a keen intelligence and a soul full of ardor, which enabled him in a short time to make rapid progress in the knowledge of grammar and letters.

At the age of seven, Vincent entered the clerical state and was even provided with an ecclesiastical benefice. At twelve, his mind was so fully developed as to enable him to penetrate into the difficulties of philosophy, and he devoted two years to that abstract study. In fine, he commenced in his fourteenth year his theological course and applied himself to this latter science until the time when he began to think seriously of determining the state of life to which the voice of God called him. At this period of his life, the virtues of the youth had in no way slackened. Their growth, on the contrary, was visible, for grace is never weakened in a soul which faithfully responds to its advances. It was his custom to assist daily at Mass, and his greatest delight was to serve the priest. His prayers were long and fervent. He had a tender devotion to Our Lord's Passion. He said habitually the Little Office of the Cross, to which he added that of the Blessed Virgin. He fasted regularly on Wednesday and Friday every week. His tenderness for the poor led him into a thousand kinds of good works which charity suggested to him. But what we wish chiefly to remark in our Saint are the dispositions which he manifested from his earliest years for his future calling to the Apostolate.

When yet a child, Vincent would commit to memory the leading points of the sermons at which he assisted and repeat them to his family around the domestic hearth. Frequently drawing his schoolfellows away from their games, he would gather them around him; then, mounting a hillock or fence, he would recite to them with earnestness, grace and unction whatever his recollection inspired him with, imitating the gestures and movements of the preachers whom he most admired. He continued the same practices as he grew up. Thus, during the years of his boyhood, he accomplished much good among the youth of his own age by speaking to them of God, of the soul and of Heaven. His example stamped on them a living impression. All looked upon him as a Saint, so much did the grace of miracles appear to increase with his years. Many attempted to imitate his virtues and to walk in his footsteps, whom he lovingly directed by his good counsels.[5]

Chapter 2

St. Vincent Ferrer Receives the Habit of the Friar Preachers—His Novitiate and Profession.

OUR Saint having now attained his eighteenth year, the moment had arrived when it behooved him to decide on the sort of life that should best suit his own tastes and the inspirations of grace. His father forestalled him in this by the following proposal: "My son," said he, "I leave you full and entire liberty, and be assured of this: I shall place no obstacle to the accomplishment of your will. Nevertheless," he added, "I would counsel you to embrace the religious life in the Order of the Friar Preachers, for such, in effect, seems to me to be God's Will when I reflect on the signs that preceded your birth." And at the same time he related to him in detail the marvelous testimonies that had been manifested and the interpretation which their relation, the Bishop, had put upon them.

Vincent replied without a moment's deliberation: "My father, you have anticipated my wishes, and I thank Our Lord for having inspired you with the thought to propose that which is the most agreeable to me. I have no longing after the riches and pleasures and honors of this life; my love, thoughts and resolutions are centered on God. I am, therefore, determined to follow His divine call to the Dominican family; and now I desire nothing more except my mother's consent and your joint blessing, that I may go in peace to serve God in the retreat which His voice clearly indicates to me." At these words his father embraced him with tears of tender compassion, and under the influence of that sweet emotion they went to find Constance, who also shed an abundance of tears—not of sorrow, but of holy joy.

"My beloved child," she cried, "what you are about to do is what I have always longed for on your part. I have frequently asked this favor of God, and now He has heard me. Oh, happy event for you and for us! We ought to congratulate each other: you, because you are about to withdraw yourself from the miseries of this life; we, because we have obtained from Our Lord the accomplishment of our most cherished desires. May God fill you, my child, with every blessing. As for myself and your father, we most willingly give you ours to the end of your life."

On the morning following that happy day, William Ferrer himself conducted his son to the

Convent of the Friar Preachers at Valencia. This was on the 2nd of February in the year 1367. The Prior of the Convent was apprised that same night by a miraculous vision of the precious conquest which the Order was about to make. St. Dominic appeared to him holding the youthful postulant by the hand. It seemed to him that Vincent, all inflamed with fervor, said to him, "Father, behold me at your feet to become one of your religious." At the same time, his conductor added, "Receive him; he shall be your brother and my son." The Prior, recognizing St. Dominic by the star which shone on his forehead, threw himself at his feet, when instantly all disappeared. There remained in his heart an ardent wish to see the speedy accomplishment of the vision with which he had been favored, and he was fully consoled when, on the following morning, our Saint, accompanied by his father, cast himself at his feet and humbly asked to receive the holy habit, affirming that his sole motive for the step he was taking was to obey the voice of God, who called him to serve Him under the glorious standard of St. Dominic.[1]

Who shall describe the joy felt by the man of God to whom this request was addressed, when he heard a young man, so accomplished, imploring with such earnestness and humility the habit of the Friar Preachers? His convent and the whole order were about to be enriched with an incomparable treasure. He experienced then a sentiment akin to that of the holy and aged Simeon, whose high privilege it was to receive in the Temple, in the name of the Almighty, the presentation of the Child Jesus, made by Mary and Joseph. This was on the day of the solemnity commemorative of that mystery. There was, then, a striking similarity in the offering. Vincent offered himself sponta- neously to the sacrifice of the religious life, while his parents accompanied the pious victim. There was even a likeness in the reception. For as the angels, the ministers of the sanctuary, the widows of the Temple and the holy people of Jersualem shared the divine joy of Simeon, so also may it be said that the religious of the convent, the friends of the Saint, his family and the entire city of Valen- cia were associated in the joy of the venerable head of the community, and united with him in thanksgiving to God for this inestimable benefit. We may well imagine that there would be but one voice for the admission of the postulant.

The day of his clothing was fixed for the 5th of February, the Feast of the glorious virgin St. Agatha—a day worthy of eternal memory to the inhabitants of the city. It was 128 years after the Convent of St. Dominic had been established. The Order was then governed by a Vicar-General named Father Elias of Toulouse. The Dominican province of Aragon had at its head Blessed James

Dominic de Collioure, and the Prior of the Convent of Valencia was the Venerable Father Beranger de Gelasio.[2]

From the first moment of his novitiate, Vincent felt so forcibly the grace which God had bestowed upon him in calling him into Religion, that he ceased not to thank Heaven and to kiss with ardor and indescribable contentment the white woolen in which he was clothed. In the convent which he had entered, there were many religious whose lives might well have served him as an example. But his generous soul chose a model even more perfect. He resolved to make his life a close imitation of that of St. Dominic; and that he might the more readily understand his actions, he began to read, with singular interest, the life of that great patriarch.

It was then especially that he learned to distinguish the true character of the Friar Preacher—as he afterwards explained in his sermons—a character which consists in angelic purity, perfect obedience and divine poverty; and not in remaining in a monastery in a state of immobility, shut up in a cell like the anchorites of old, but to go to preach the Gospel throughout the world, after the example of Christ, the Apostles and the holy Founder of the Order. "For it is for this," he added, "that the Order of the Friar Preachers was instituted."

Vincent penetrated in a wonderful manner the deep meaning of each of the characteristics of the life of the blessed Father. As a proof of this, we need only cite the interpretation which he gave of the celebrated vision in which St. Dominic appeared crowned with glory and ascending to Heaven by means of two ladders. "Our Order," he observed, "does not lead its subjects to Heaven by the ladder of the contemplative life alone, nor by that of the active life only, but it enables them to ascend to the conquest of Paradise by means of both. They who are in the simple monastic state reach Heaven by the ladder of contemplation; and it is by ascending that of the active life that the military orders arrive at the possession of their country. But the children of St. Dominic must have a foot on each, by uniting the exercises of prayer and study to the work of apostolic preaching." This fact alone enables us to judge with what clearness of mind our Saint knew his destiny and the duties which it involved. The young novice was ever faithful to this light, and to the day of his death he reflected in his person the perfect image of St. Dominic.

During the course of his novitiate, Vincent applied himself exclusively, according to the spirit of the rule, to the exercises of the interior life. Never did he omit any of the prayers or mortifications which he imposed on himself. And even though the Dominican Constitutions do not bind under sin, yet he observed their smallest details with as great exactitude as if he had been bound to their fulfillment under pain of grievous sin. At choir and at recreation he was the first; and he would never absent himself from any of the common duties to satisfy his own particular devotion. He obeyed everyone with profound humility. His sweetness and modesty rendered him amiable to all, and the affability of his character caused his conversation to be sought by every member of the novitiate. He was the youngest in the convent, but was already looked upon as the first in sanctity.

Three months of his novitiate had elapsed when a trial painful to the heart of a son beset his vocation. Vincent was called upon to resist the tears of his own mother. Constance Miguel, going to the convent one day, asked to see her son. When he appeared, she represented to him, with tears, the following considerations: that she could not live without him; that it was easy for him, her son, to sanctify himself among the secular clergy; besides, his family stood in need of the revenues of his ecclesiastical benefice, which obliged him to renounce his religious profession. He must therefore leave the convent and return to the world.

Sorrowfully affected by these entreaties, Vincent nevertheless answered his mother with invincible firmness: "You were willing that I should enter the cloister, and you gave me your blessing when I left you. Why then shall I go back? I shall ever remember the saying of St. Bernard: 'He who leaves the convent to return to the world quits the company of angels to join that of the devil!' I would beseech you then, my dear mother, to return to your first sentiments; let us view the things of this world with the eye of faith, and let us value them now as we shall wish to have valued them at the hour of death. One thing only is necessary, and it behooves each of us to accomplish his salvation in the manner that God ordains."

These words, affording Constance no hope of persuading her son to renounce his vocation, filled her with sadness, and she returned to her home in great grief. But God did not abandon her in that trying circumstance. As she approached her house, she saw a poor person who, saluting her courteously, said, "Madam, why are you sorrowful? Have you forgotten the miraculous barkings which you heard when you bore Vincent in your womb? Has your husband's prophetic dream passed from your memory? Do you not remember how the Bishop of Valencia interpreted those mysterious signs and how you predicted that your son would one day be a Friar Preacher? Would you now frustrate the accomplishment of the Divine Will?" These words consoled Constance and drew forth her tears. Before long, she recognized in that poor person a messenger from Heaven, for going into her house to get an alms to recompense him with for his good words, she no longer found him on her return either at the threshold or in the street.

The year of probation passed by without further interruption. Then the young novice, who had been the edification of the community, was unanimously admitted to the solemn profession of his vows. He pronounced them in the hands of Father Matthew Benincasa, who that year was Prior of the Convent of Valencia. Such was the joy of the brethren, that every year afterwards, till the destruction of the convent, they celebrated the anniversary of that happy day.[3]

—SECTION TWO—

FROM THE SAINT'S RELIGIOUS
PROFESSION TO HIS CALL TO A
MIRACULOUS APOSTOLATE.
1368-1398.

Chapter 3

Studies of St. Vincent Ferrer—His Profound
Learning—His Great Piety during His Course of
Studies and Scholastic Labors.

HAD St. Vincent died in his novitiate or
shortly after his profession in religion, he
would doubtless have merited to be venerated on
the altar, like the Blessed Peter of Luxemburg,
who died at the age of eighteen, and the youthful
confessors Aloysius de Gonzaga and Stanislaus
Kostka, who are the glory and ornament of the
Society of Jesus. But Divine Providence was
pleased to increase in a high degree, by a long
life of merit, the beauty of the crown of glory
reserved for him. Vincent bore the sacred yoke of
the religious and apostolic life for more than 50
years. During that long space of half a century,
he united with perfect fidelity and undaunted
constancy the austerities of the cloister with the
fatigues of the ministry of souls. Hence we may
judge of the merits accumulated by this intrepid
workman, and of the immense harvest of glory
which he gathered to the end of his career. From

the moment that he saw himself irrevocably engaged in the Order of Preachers, he resolved to apply himself without relaxation to three things: assiduous prayer, the study of theology and Holy Scripture. These form the triple duty of a Friar Preacher who desires to labor fruitfully for the good of souls. For without prayer, he can neither sanctify himself nor others; without the study of theology and of the Scripture, he lacks the knowledge which is indispensable to his occupying the pulpit with becoming dignity.

There exists in the Order the admirable custom that students, in whom is discovered a more than ordinary capacity, should be employed in teaching others as soon as they have finished their own studies. This professorial employment is even necessary to enable them to advance in the order of academic degrees, which, despite a searching examination, cannot be obtained unless that condition is fulfilled. One can readily understand that such a system is well suited to form solid preachers; for an accomplished student who has spent ten, fifteen or twenty years—whether in studying or in teaching philosophy, theology and Holy Scripture—ought to be at the end of that term, trained to all the difficulties of science, and admirably qualified to explain to the people the truths of dogmatic and moral teaching. St. Vincent passed through all those different stages till he reached the highest grade of all, that of Master in Theology.

On leaving the novitiate, Vincent's superiors assigned him the duties of teaching logic and philosophy in the same Convent of Valencia, and he devoted himself to that duty to the satisfaction of the students who attended his lectures. Many students from the city desired to hear him speak, that they might listen to a professor whose science was only surpassed by his sanctity.

Three years later, Vincent was sent to Lerida to teach. He remained there two years, and his lectures bore the same fruitful results as at Valencia. When his superiors judged him to be sufficiently versed in the subtleties of metaphysics, they wished him to apply himself to the special study of the Holy Scripture, and for that purpose they assigned him in the year 1372 to the Convent of Barcelona, where he resided three years. Here he devoted himself with incredible ardor to the study of the Sacred Writings; and that he might increase his knowledge of the Old Testament, he learned Hebrew. St. Raymund of Pennafort, the third General of the Order, had instituted in Spain many schools of that language for the sake of converting the Jews, who were numerous in the country and for whose conversion a knowledge of the Hebrew tongue was indispensable. He had too great a zeal for the salvation of souls not to enter into the views of St. Raymund. He acquired such a perfect knowledge of Hebrew that he was able to quote to the Jews every text of the Old Testament, and to refute the absurd doctrines of the Talmud and the lying stories with which that book abounds. It is thought that he also knew the Greek and Arabic tongues. Three years were devoted by the Saint to the exclusive study of Scripture, and one more year to teaching physics in the same Convent of Barcelona. In the year 1376 he returned to Valencia, where he renewed his fervor by means of a spiritual retreat. Then, in the year 1377, he was sent by the chapter of his province to Toulouse, and in the following year to Paris. In both cities he continued to perfect himself in the divine sciences by teaching them to others. His sojourn at Paris lasted only a year, after which he returned again to Valencia and took charge of the theological course for six consecutive years. In the year 1388, his superiors sent him to Lerida, to receive the degree of Doctor of Theology in the celebrated university of that city. When they laid this command upon him, he humbly submitted himself to it, not to gratify a vain ambition, but to render himself capable of doing greater good in the Church. He was then in his thirty-eighth year, and had been a priest only seven years. While he stayed at Barcelona, he composed two treatises, one on *Dialectical Suppositions*, the other on the *Nature of the Universal*. His contemporaries speak of them with much praise, but these works are not extant in our times.[1]

Study and teaching are rocks that are sometimes fatal to the piety of those engaged in them. St. Vincent knew how to avoid those perils. Making the science of perfection his first care, he suffered not the fervor which inflamed his soul to grow cold in the midst of scholastic speculations. Study was to him a continual exercise of devotion; not only did he refer it to God with perfect purity of intention, but he even pictured to himself as hearing from the mouth of Divine Wisdom Itself all that he read. Whenever any difficulty presented itself, and especially in passages that were most obscure, he was accustomed to ask of Jesus, as his heavenly Master, that intelligence and light of which he stood in need. He frequently raised his eyes from his books and fixed them lovingly on the wounds of his crucified Lord; for some moments he would draw from that source of ineffable sweetness the delights which inundated his soul and immediately afterwards resume his reading. At other times, leaving his desk and casting himself on his knees, he poured forth to Heaven an ardent prayer with sighs and lamentations, beseeching God to infuse into his soul new flames of love. He thus passed from study to prayer, and from prayer to study, and each of these occupations developed at the same time his science and piety.

Besides the ascetic exercises to which he applied himself in his cell, he devoted a considerable portion of the night to prayer in the church. There especially, even more than in his cell, he was favored with a multitude of heavenly visions and singular graces, which maintained his soul in fervor and daily increased his devotion. One night, while praying before the crucifix and meditating on the sufferings of Jesus, contemplating the wounds in His hands and His feet and His sacred side, he was moved to tears, and in accents of tender compassion he exclaimed, "O Lord, you have suffered on the cross!" The crucifix, turning the head to the left where the Saint prayed, replied, "Yes, Vincent, I have borne all these sufferings, and even more." This miraculous crucifix, having the head in the position which it assumed when uttering these words, has been religiously preserved to this day.[2]

When he had completed the thirty-first year of his age, Vincent was promoted to the holy priesthood. The ancient canons required clerics to have attained that number of years before being advanced to the priestly dignity, and at that period this point of law was generally observed in the Order of St. Dominic. How did the Saint celebrate his first Mass? In what manner did he prepare himself for that great act? The historians of his life give us no clue to this. Yet we may judge of the fervor which he employed in that solemn act by that which the Sacrifice of the Altar inspired him throughout the course of his life. "The Mass," he observes in one of his sermons, "is the most sublime work of contemplation that can be." He never performed that divine function without shedding abundant tears of piety and holy joy, especially from the commencement of the Canon to the Communion. He might have been looked upon as another St. Dominic celebrating the Sacred Mysteries.

The perfection of his monastic observance increased daily with his piety. The Constitutions of the Order were the object of his special attention; he observed them with the minuteness and interior spirit which they exact on the part of him who is a true and faithful servant of God. To understand his sublime sentiments respecting the sanctity of the state which he had embraced, the obligations of the religious life, and the virtues of the soul which, renouncing the world, desires to live only for God and the salvation of its neighbors; to gain an insight into the numberless secrets which the Saint discovered in order to accomplish in the highest degree of perfection the commonest acts of life, such as repose, sleeping, eating, conversation and recreation, it suffices to read his *Treatise on the Spiritual Life*, one of his few works that have escaped the wreck of time. There we shall find the living portraiture of him who wrote it. St. Vincent has painted himself therein, and has doubtless given us a true idea of his own perfection. The author first lays down a number of general rules; then he enters in detail into the daily exercises which fill up the life of a religious. He next enumerates the various motives which ought to engage him to strive without ceasing toward true perfection. Poverty, silence and purity of heart are, according to him, the necessary foundations of a spiritual life. He further explains, with charming simplicity, the manner of regulating the body at table, in the dormitory and at choir. The advice he gives on how to avoid softness and excess in the various practices of mortification displays a remarkable depth of wisdom. As to the labors employed in the acquisition of science, we ought, he says, to study as it becomes Christians, to transform, so to speak, study into prayer. In the same work is found useful advice on the subject of false revelations which ensnare spiritual men. In short, St. Vincent prescribes a method of preaching, recommending above all, simplicity, and even a sort of naïveté which the preacher may indulge in with a view to rendering himself more intelligible to his listeners. All these different counsels were the fruits of St. Vincent's own reflections, experience and daily practice.

The evil spirit tempted him in a thousand ways

to lead him into grievous faults, or at least to relax the ardor of his zeal in regard to good. We find a record of two apparitions of Satan in the *Spiritual Instruction*—for the second Friday before the Saint's Feast and in that for the eighth day of his novena. But the Saint always victoriously escaped the plots of Hell.

Chapter 4

First Preachings of St. Vincent Ferrer—
Continuation of the Saint's Preaching until His
Definitive Call to Avignon.

IT was while he sojourned at Barcelona—
during the year 1372 to 1375—that our Saint
began to preach publicly to the people. He was
then only in deacon's orders. Such was the fervor,
unctions and eloquence of his discourses, that the
multitude was deeply moved. Numberless conversions signalized his first feat of arms in the apostolic warfare. People flocked, not only from the
neighboring cities, but from more than ten leagues
around [approximately 30 miles], that they might
hear him. So great was the concourse of people
that the largest churches were insufficient to hold
them; and to satisfy their devotion, Vincent was
obliged to preach to them in the public squares.

A remarkable incident occurred which tended
greatly to establish his authority among the people. For a whole year Barcelona was desolated by
a frightful famine; the wheat failed, and efforts
were made on every side to supply the deficiency,

but in vain. Human succor was no longer available. The inhabitants had recourse to public prayers and processions to obtain from God deliverance from the plague.

One day, in the beginning of the spring of 1375, a large procession arrived in one of the city squares, and Vincent addressed the multitude with a fervent exhortation to repentence. He represented to them how a forgetfulness of the divine law brought upon Christian people the terrible scourge of famine. Then he exhorted them to place their confidence in God, who would not permit His children to perish in the midst of the evils which He sent upon them to correct and sanctify them. Then he suddenly exclaimed: "Have courage and be glad, my brethren, for this very night two vessels will arrive in this port laden with wheat, which will supply you with abundant provisions."

But on that particular day, and for many days previously, the sea had been so terribly agitated that it seemed impossible for any vessel to live in so great a storm. Only a few of his hearers believed in the prophecy; the greater number murmured against the preacher, taxing him with imprudence, boasting and vainglory. His own brethren, to whom these complaints were made, cautioned him to be more guarded in his speech for the future. Vincent received the admonition with sincere humility. Then, without losing his serenity of soul, he spent the rest of the day at the foot of the altar, beseeching God to pardon the want of faith in the people and not to withhold from them the succor which He destined for them. Great indeed was the surprise of those whom the Saint's words had irritated when, toward evening, two vessels freighted with wheat entered the port of Barcelona, which were followed in a few days by twenty others bearing similar cargoes from the ports of Flanders. At the sight of such an abundant supply of provisions, they acknowledged the truth of the Saint's prophecy, repented of having murmured against him and sought to repair the injury done to him by listening to him in the future with perfect docility.[1]

According to his biographers, this man of God, during his stay in Paris in the year 1379, was not content with instructing the young religious committed to his care, but he also announced the Divine Word to the people. His preaching in the French metropolis bore the same marvelous fruits which accompanied it in Spain. His unrivaled eloquence was not only listened to with keen admiration, but with compunction of heart and tears of repentance. Each of his discourses was followed by numerous conversions.

Valencia, which gave him birth, was, however, the principal scene of his success at this period of his life. An eager multitude thronged around his pulpit, and he wrought in souls prodigies of grace and sanctification. When he was promoted to the priesthood, his success increased still more. He was immediately permitted to use the faculties which he received to absolve people from sin. Having begun then to hear Confessions, he reaped himself in great part the fruit of the Gospel seed which he had sown for a long time by his preaching. In this useful ministry, he consolidated marvelously the immense good which he had begun in his public preaching. Moreover, the inhabitants of Valencia were not content with seeing in him an enlightened guide in the path of Christian perfection, a skillful physician of souls, but they considered him a universal adviser and the refuge of all who were afflicted. All classes of people had recourse to him. The common people and the nobility equally consulted him as an oracle and obeyed with docility his decisions, which were replete with tact and justice.

It was then that, jealous of his success, Hell invented many scandals against the Saint, which we withhold for the present, and shall relate only the following.

One night, a wicked old man went to the house of a woman of ill fame, disguised in the black mantle of the Friar Preachers. He made great promises to her, adding that his name was Vincent

Ferrer, but the woman never saw him again. She then carried her complaint to the warden of the city, who happened that year to be Boniface Ferrer, brother of the Saint. The warden on hearing her complaint suspected it to be a monstrous falsehood, inspired through hatred or envy. The Dominicans were to traverse a part of the city in procession. Boniface, accompanied by several witnesses, stationed himself with the plaintiff, in a house, where they could see all the friars pass. He then asked her to point out to him the individual of whom she complained. She could not distinguish him. He pointed to his own brother. "Is he the person?" he asked.

"Oh!" she exclaimed, "he is a Saint, I have sometimes heard him preach."

"That Saint is Vincent Ferrer," he said, "and I am his brother. You have been imposed upon, in order to calumniate him."

Still, Boniface could find no rest until he had discovered the guilty person. He then summoned him before several judges and obliged him to ask pardon of the Saint. This is the old man of whom mention is made in the *Spiritual Instruction* for the fifth day of the novena.[2]

St. Vincent had been a Master in Theology for two years and was engaged in preaching to the inhabitants of Valencia and other cities of Aragon when Cardinal Peter de Luna passed through that city. This prelate had been canon and provost of the cathedral. The Church was at that moment unhappily divided between the papal claimants of Avignon and those of Rome. Peter de Luna went into Spain in the role of Apostolic Legate, to induce that country to accept the authority of Clement VII, then Pope of Avignon. He had already heard Vincent spoken of and was not surprised at the unanimous praise which his countrymen heaped upon him. He himself had occasion to judge how much the Saint merited the high esteem which surrounded him, and he resolved to attach Vincent to himself during his legation in Spain and then to present him at the court of Clement VII of Avignon. Venerating in his person an Ambassador of the Holy See, Vincent consented to accompany him and followed him to Salamanca, where the King of Castile then was. In his journey, his zeal did not allow him to remain silent, and he preached in the various cities through which he passed. This was not without its fruit, for in Valladolid he converted a Jewish Rabbi, who, being promoted to the priesthood, afterwards became Bishop of Carthagena. He also brought to the Faith, or to a reformation of life, a multitude of Jews, infidels and bad Catholics. When Peter de Luna had terminated his legation, he invited Vincent to accompany him to the court of Clement VII; but the Saint, not considering himself bound to yield to de Luna's desires and seeing that he could accomplish greater good to souls, preferred to continue his preaching in Castile.

On his return to Valencia, he was nominated, contrary to his wishes, confessor to Violante, Queen of Aragon, consort of John I. He directed this princess with extreme prudence. She was a woman of a lively disposition and of varied talents, but imperious, greedy for power and desirous of having the whole world at her feet. She governed her royal spouse, whose whole conduct was the result of her counsels. Yet she submitted with docility to the enlightened direction of St. Vincent, who tried to inspire her with contempt for the world and a love of heavenly things. The veneration which she conceived for her holy director was doubtless the means which Providence made use of to improve her. Vincent was not a cowardly flatterer in her regard, always ready to close his eyes to the faults of his penitent. An example related in the *Spiritual Instructions* for the seventh Friday before the Saint's Feast shows that he knew how to reprimand her when she deserved it.

On the 1st of July in the year 1391, the Jews of Valencia were led, by various miraculous circumstances, to ask to be instructed in the Christian Faith. The Bishop of that city appointed Vincent to instruct them. The greater part were converted, and their synagogue was transformed into a church dedicated to St. Christopher.

Shortly after this harvest of souls, Vincent returned to Catalonia and went to the court of John I, who resided for a time in that province. He was made a Councillor of State and Grand Almoner to the King of Aragon, besides being Confessor to the Queen Consort. He remained at court till the death of that prince, which occurred in the year 1396. These new honors were no hindrance to the Saint's apostolic zeal. He preached daily and with equal success in different places, including Cordova, whose inhabitants conceived so high a veneration for him that they cut in pieces his religious mantle and shared them with each other as sacred relics.

But while he thus exercised the ardor of his zeal in Aragon, Clement VII died. Peter de Luna was elected Pope by the Cardinals of Avignon and took the name of Benedict XIII. Two years following his election to the Supreme Pontificate, Benedict nominated his confessor, the Carmelite Jerome of Ochoa, to the Bishopric of Elne, in Roussillon, and chose Vincent to replace him as his confessor. He dispatched messengers with letters to request him to come without delay to Avignon. The Saint obeyed, without replying to so formal an injunction, and hastened to where Benedict, whom he regarded as Pope, called him. While journeying there, he ceased not to preach to the people in the cities where he was obliged to stay.

Arrived at the court of Avignon (this was in 1396), St. Vincent was surrounded with the most flattering marks of esteem. Benedict, desirous of attaching the Saint to himself by other titles than that of Confessor, nominated him Master of the Sacred Palace, Grand Penitentiary and his own private chaplain. In the midst of these exalted honors, the humble religious interrupted not his customary exercises of piety, his assiduous study of the Sacred Writings and his preaching to the people. His exemplary life added great weight to his words. Amidst the luxury of the Papal Court, he practiced the same austerities as if he had been in a regular convent—observing the same fasts and prolonging equally his prayers and watchings. He preached less frequently, doubtless on account of his functions, but it was always with the same abundant fruit. At his voice, a crowd of sinners, weeping over their past iniquities, began a life of sincere penitence and repaired with edifying piety the scandals they had given to the world.[3]

—SECTION THREE—

THE MIRACULOUS APOSTOLATE
OF ST. VINCENT FERRER.
1398-1419.

Chapter 5

Christ Miraculously Calls the Saint to an
Extraordinary Apostolate in the Church—State
of Christianity at the Epoch when
St. Vincent Received His Divine Mission.

————————

NO sooner had he been installed in his new
dignities, than the Saint sought by every
means at his command to bring about a union of
the Faithful under one Supreme Head. He daily
implored his illustrious penitent to relinquish his
claims to the Papacy, in order to do away with the
monstrous phenomenon of two heads over one
body. At his urging, a large council of prelates,
theologians and canonists was gathered together
to discuss the relative claims of the contending
parties. With fair speeches, Benedict showed himself well disposed, but artfully eluded all negotia-
tion that was likely to terminate the difficulty, in
consequence of which a number of his own cardinals abandoned his cause. Seeing that his efforts
were useless to induce the Pope to lay aside the
tiara, St. Vincent was seized with deep sorrow. He
could no longer witness the evils that were crush-

ing the Church without being moved to tears. His residence at the pontifical court was now a tax upon him, and he obtained permission to retire to a convent of his Order at Avignon. Such was his sorrow that he fell grievously ill; no remedies could diminish the intensity of the fever that consumed him; and for twelve days he lay at death's door. On the eve of the Feast of St. Francis, October 3rd, 1396, a crisis ensued which greatly alarmed those who surrounded his bed of suffering, for they believed that his last hour had come. But God was at that moment pleased to verify in His servant what He had spoken in the Book of Job: "When thou shalt think thyself consumed, thou shalt rise as the day star." (*Job* 11:17). Suddenly the Saint's cell was flooded with a celestial light. Our Lord, accompanied by a multitude of angels and the glorious patriarchs, Dominic and Francis, presented Himself to the sufferer, saying: "Arise, and be consoled; the schism shall soon be at an end, when men have ceased from their iniquities. Arise, then, and go to preach against vice, for this have I specially chosen thee. Exhort sinners to repentance, for My judgment is at hand." Then Our Lord promised him three favors: that he would be confirmed in grace, that he would be victorious over all the persecutions raised against him, that in all his conflicts the Divine assistance would never fail him, and that after having

preached the judgment throughout the greater part
of Europe, with immense fruit to souls, he would
terminate his life holily in a distant country.
Finally, He instructed Vincent in all that related to
the exercise of his apostolic ministry. His biographers have not supplied us with details, but it is
easy to conceive them from the admirable order
invariably followed by the new Apostle in his
miraculous calling. Ceasing to speak to the Saint,
Our Lord, in token of His love, touched him on the
face with His right hand and said to him a second
time, "My Vincent, arise." He then disappeared.
The Divine touch produced its effect. Vincent suddenly felt himself cured, and his heart was filled
with ineffable consolation.

This marvelous apparition, recorded by the old-
est biographers of the Saint, is all the more worthy
of belief inasmuch as St. Vincent himself confirmed it in a letter which he wrote to Benedict
XIII fifteen years later. Writing to him in the third
person, he says: "A religious was grievously ill,
and he lovingly besought God to cure him and to
enable him to preach His Divine Word frequently
and ardently, as he had been accustomed to do.
While he was in prayer and fell asleep, St.
Dominic and St. Francis appeared to him, praying
at the feet of Jesus Christ and earnestly supplicat-
ing Our Lord. After they had finished their prayer,
Jesus Christ appeared with them to the religious,

who lay stretched upon his bed of pain. He
touched him on the cheek with His sacred hand as
if caressing him, and at the same time made him
clearly understand, in words which the soul alone
heard, that he should traverse the world, preaching
as an Apostle, as St. Dominic and St. Francis had
done, and that his preaching, before the coming of
the Antichrist, would be to mankind a merciful
occasion of repentance and conversion. At the
touch of Our Lord's hand, this religious was completely cured of his malady. He at once joyfully
undertook the apostolic legation with which he
had been divinely entrusted. Divine Providence
was pleased to confirm his mission, not only by
many miracles, as He had done with that of
Moses, but also by the authority of Holy Scripture,
as in the case of St. John the Baptist, because he
had need of these powerful helps, on account of
the difficulty of his enterprise and the weakness of
his own testimony."[1]

The cell in which St. Vincent received
so remarkable a favor and such a miraculous mission was converted into a chapel, which became
the object of great devotion. It was destroyed in
the French Revolution, together with the Convent
which enclosed it.

On the morning following his miraculous cure,
Vincent presented himself before the Pope to
obtain permission to leave the city for the purpose

of preaching the Gospel throughout the kingdoms of Europe. But Benedict, unwilling to part with one whose popularity would doubtless benefit his own cause, still detained him at his court. The Saint humbly obeyed, well knowing that particular revelations ought always to be submitted to the control of God's Church, and deferred to a more favorable opportunity the execution of his project. For two years longer he discharged the duties of Master of the Sacred Palace and served with heroic patience and exemplary fidelity him whom he looked upon as the veritable Vicar of Jesus Christ. To secure for the future his attachment to the cause of the Popes of Avignon, the bishopric of Lerida and a cardinal's hat were offered him. These honors Vincent courteously but firmly declined, saying, "It behooves me to execute the order which I have received from God, for God has commanded me to preach the judgment to all nations." One day, feeling sad at the resistance which Benedict still offered to his ardent desires, he prayed in tears before his crucifix and offered to God the sorrow of his soul. Our Lord consoled him with these words: *"Vade adhuc expectabo te"* ["Come, I shall still await thee"]—He clearly understood that he should no longer resist His solicitations. The Pontiff then allowed him to set out on his apostolic mission throughout Europe, and for that purpose he granted him the fullest powers, which were afterwards confirmed by the Council of Constance and by Pope Martin V.

St. Vincent began his new apostolate at Avignon on the 25th of November, 1398.

The Church of God had at that time a pressing need for the voice of an apostle, the voice of a Saint, to rescue it from the deplorable state in which it existed. There arose, in the year 1378, a schism which divided the allegiance of the Faithful between two contending Pontiffs, and as if to complete the evil, a third rival sprang up in 1409, who asserted an equal claim to the supreme dignity of the Papacy. These unhappy divisions cooled by degrees the fervor of Christian people and encouraged others in the commission of every type of crime with the hope of impunity. The wickedness of men had reached its summit. "No, I do not believe," exclaimed St. Vincent in one of his discourses, "that there ever existed in the world so much pomp and vanity, so much impurity, as at the present day; to find in the world's history an epoch so criminal, we must go back to the days of Noe and the universal deluge. The inns in the cities and villages are filled with persons of abandoned character; they are so numerous that the entire world is infected by them . . . Avarice and usury increase under the disguised name of contracts. Simony reigns among the clergy, envy among the religious. Gluttony prevails to such an extent in every rank of social life that the fasts of Lent, the vigils and Ember Days, are no longer observed. . . . In a word, vice is held in such great honour that those who prefer the service of God to that of the world are held up to scorn as useless and unworthy members of society."

But the worst feature of all in this unhappy state of affairs was that the pastors of souls, drawn from the path of duty by the schism and its consequences, no longer labored with the necessary vigilance to reform their people. The Mohammedans and Jews, especially in Spain, instigated by the spirit of evil, made frightful havoc among souls by infecting the country parishes as well as the cities with their superstitions, errors and wicked example. The devil let loose upon the earth numerous heretics: For example Wycliff and his noxious disciples, John Hus and Jerome of Prague, who were justly condemned by the Council of Constance. Idolatry even ventured to raise its head once more on the shores of Europe and threatened to bear off in triumph its deluded followers. There were but few preachers of the Gospel, while men versed in spiritual science were rarely to be met with. St. Vincent regarded this dearth of apostolic laborers as one of the greatest calamities of the age and bitterly laments it in his *Treatise on the Spiritual Life.* Naturally, drawn into a state of indifference and evil, what was there to prevent men from becoming more and more corrupt, when they more frequently heard the voice which led them into depravity than the voice which ought to have incited them to good? The heretics profited by these evil dispositions to so broadcast their errors among the faithful. The mountainous districts, into which preachers seldom went, became the principal theaters of their fatal exploits.

Sin had acquired so strong a hold upon the world, the fervor of the good had become so relaxed and the crimes of the wicked had risen to such an excess, that God's patient forbearance with His creatures was nearly worn out. The only remedy that could stem the torrent of iniquity was a universal repentance, capable of appeasing the Just and Sovereign Judge. Hence, as of old the Lord sent the prophet Jonas to Nineve to convert its inhabitants by threatening them with God's anger, so at this epoch He sent His faithful servant Vincent into the whole world, that he might preach the near approach of the terrible judgment; that, filling souls with a wholesome fear, they might open their eyes to see their danger, abandon their evil habits, embrace the yoke of penance and thus avert the just chastisements of Heaven which their crimes merited.

It is in this light that Pope Pius II exhibits St. Vincent Ferrer to our view in the Bull of his canonization. We read therein these remarkable words: "In the countries of the West the number of Jews and infidels increased, who by their wealth and their culture of letters exercised a fatal influence. The Last Day, the terrible Day of Judgment, was almost forgotten, but Divine Providence was pleased to restore and beautify His Church by illustrious men. At a favorable moment He sent into the world, for the salvation of the faithful, Vincent of Valencia, of the Order of Friar Preachers, a skillful professor of sacred theology. He professed all knowledge of the eternal Gospel. Like a vigorous athlete, he rushed to combat the errors of the Jews, the Saracens and other infidels; he was the Angel of the Apocalypse, flying through the heavens to announce the day of the Last Judgment, to evangelize the inhabitants of the earth, to sow the seeds of salvation among all nations, tribes, peoples and tongues, and to point out the way of eternal life"[2]

"These words," observes Father Teoli, "perfectly express what St. Vincent Ferrer was during the last twenty years of his life—an Apostle,[3] and a great Apostle." The celebrated Louis of Granada boldly affirms of him: "After the first Apostles, Vincent is, of all apostolic men, he who has gathered most fruit in God's vineyard." His contemporaries assert that he frequently had 80,000 listeners.[4] He was already forty-nine years old when Our Lord named him His legate to reform the world; and for the space of twenty years, he acquitted himself of that sacred charge, traversing the whole of Europe and converting to the Faith in each city Jews, infidels, heretics and sinners by the thousands.

Chapter 6

St. Vincent's Mode of Life During His
Miraculous Apostolate—The Method Employed
by the Saint in Preaching.

ALTHOUGH provided with the fullest authorizations on the part of the Sovereign Pontiffs, St. Vincent would never preach in any place without the blessing and consent of the Bishop of the diocese and the permission of the local Superiors of his Order. He imposed on himself the inflexible rule to travel always on foot, despite the distance, the difficulties of the route and the severity of the seasons. It was only toward the latter years of his life that a painful wound in one of his legs obliged him to ride. But even in this he observed the spirit of simplicity and poverty. He refused the use of a horse and chose rather to ride on a mean ass, that he might the more resemble the Saviour of men.

Before entering into any city, he cast himself on his knees, then raising his eyes toward Heaven and shedding abundant tears, he prayed for the people to whom he was about to preach the judgment. His entry was ordinarily attended with much solemnity. The Bishop, clergy, magistrates, nobility and a numerous crowd of people came out to meet him. They conducted him under a canopy with honor equal to that of a royal personage, or rather of an apostle or an Angel. They chanted with indescribable enthusiasm hymns, psalms and sacred canticles. In the place where they met him, a cross was planted to perpetuate the memory of that happy event. So great was the concourse of people at times that it was necessary to erect a wooden barrier to protect him from the multitude who eagerly pressed around him to see him, and even to touch him. In the midst of these wondrous triumphs, his humility remained ever the same. At such moments he had incessantly in his heart and on his lips those words of the Psalmist: "Not to us, O Lord, not to us, but to Thy Name give glory" (*Psalm* 113 [2nd part]:1).

On arriving at any place, his first care was to visit the principal church, to pour forth his fervent supplications before the Blessed Sacrament and to commend to God his preaching. Then, turning to the people, he would humbly ask them to afford hospitality to those of his company who might not be able to obtain lodging at the public inns. When there was a convent of his Order in the city, Vincent always retired to it, unless the Bishop desired him to go to his palace, where he might be of greater use to the people. But in villages where his Order had no existence, he chose to reside in a monastery of friars or with the curé. On his way to his lodgings, he chanted with his companions the Litany of the Blessed Virgin or some pious prayers.

Notwithstanding the fatigues of the journey, the Saint gave himself but little repose in the house where he abode. He continued his exercises in their accustomed order; he fasted, abstained, prayed and read the Holy Scriptures. We have already observed that the Rule of the Friar Preachers does not bind under the penalty of sin, and we shall further add that, outside the convents, it admits of an almost general dispensation from the observances which constitute the monastic life; yet our Saint availed himself of no dispensation whatever, but adhered to the Rule with the fidelity of the most fervent novice. He observed all its austerities, and even added others. Thus, he constantly wore a rough hair shirt. Every night, before taking his collation, he disciplined himself to blood, and when too feeble to do this himself, he implored one of his companions, in the name of Our Lord's Passion, to render him that service and not to spare him. He allowed himself only five hours' sleep. His bed was ordinarily the hard ground or a few bundles of twigs; a stone, or a volume of the Holy Scriptures, served him for a pillow.

At daybreak, St. Vincent rose, confessed and recited a portion of the Divine Office on his knees; then he went with his companions to the church to sing Mass. At the close of that solemn function, ascending the pulpit, which was surmounted by a canopy to protect him from the burning sun and at the same time to enable his voice to reach the extremity of his audience, he yielded himself to the ardor of his zeal and expounded, with irresistible power and divine eloquence the great truths of religion.

After the sermon, he remained some time at the foot of the pulpit to bless the sick who were brought to him in large numbers and whom he often miraculously cured. A bell summoned the people at that moment and was called the *Bell of Miracles*.

When he had finished this work of charity, he retired with the priests, his companions, to hear the Confessions of those whom he had converted, and he remained thus occupied till midday, the hour of his repast. He spent the time between his frugal meal and vespers in spiritual reading or meditating in silence, and after vespers he preached again. The rest of the day was spent in hearing Confessions, or in preaching to monks, nuns or priests, wherever the Divine inspiration led him. Toward evening, he told one of his companions to ring the *Bell of Miracles*. At that well-known sound, the sick reassembled in the church to receive their health. Evening closed in with a procession of penitents, who gave themselves publicly the discipline, and with that ceremony St. Vincent terminated the daily exercises of his ministry.[1]

This prince of preachers was endowed with every oratorical quality capable of impressing the multitude. A pleasing exterior also weighed in his favor. He was of middle stature, well-proportioned, easy and dignified in manner and of handsome countenance. His tonsure was formed of rich flaxen hair, which became slightly mixed with grey toward the end of his life; his forehead was broad, majestic and calm; his large dark eyes shone with the light of intelligence and modesty. In his youth he was of a florid complexion, but his long mortifications imparted to his features an austere paleness, an unmistakeable sign of his penitential life. His appearance alone, when in the pulpit, sufficed to inspire all hearts with compunction, for his face was resplendent with sanctity and the virtues which accompanied it.

His expressive gestures were full of grace and energy, and they corresponded naturally with his words. His voice, which was as sonorous as a silver trumpet, adapted itself with marvelous effect to the necessity of the moment. When he declaimed against vice, his voice became loud and piercing and struck terror into the hearts of his hearers. When he exhorted them to a love of God, the practice of virtue or the desire of Heaven, it immediately assumed a sympathetic accent, a tender sweetness, which melted them to tears. When he spoke of Our Lord's Passion, the sorrows of His Blessed Mother, or the souls in Purgatory, that sad plaintive voice, broken at intervals by sighs, inspired deep reverence and lively compassion. The commencement of his discourse was usually marked by a grave, penetrating tone, capable of riveting the attention, while he finished in a tone that was most sweet and full of love. Frequently his countenance appeared as if on fire, but toward the end it became as white as snow.

These exterior gifts were worthily matched in our Saint by the qualities of his mind. We have already remarked in these pages that for a long space of time St. Vincent taught the sciences of philosophy and theology in the public schools. Thanks to these occupations, and to the natural brightness of his intellect, he had laid up a large store of doctrine and had acquired a powerful mode of reasoning. His happy memory crowned his facility of speech; he knew the whole of the Scriptures by heart, and the opinions of the Fathers and Doctors of the Church were most familiar to him. He fertilized this precious ground by meditation while passing from city to city, and during the night he prepared his discourse in a manner still more immediate.

But it was especially in prayer that the great Apostle of the fifteenth century found his sublime ideas, his tender sentiments and that divine unction which inflamed his words. One of his listeners, being one day enraptured by the profound doctrine which he had expounded with as much clearness as warmth, asked him from what book he drew the marvelous erudition and original ideas of his discourses. St. Vincent showed him the crucifix: "See," he said, "the book whence I gather all that I preach and in which I study my sermons." Indeed, profane literature never provided the Saint with matter for preaching. It was only the Scriptures, explained by the Fathers of the Church. Seldom did the examples and authorities of pagan authors rise to his lips. Jesus Christ has said "Preach the Gospel," but nowhere has He said, "Preach Ovid, or Virgil or Horace." Such were his principles, and they were established on reason, for as a fountain cannot rise higher than the source which feeds it, so profane teaching, coming as it does from the earth, cannot rise above the level of the earth, whereas, the Gospel enables both those who preach and those who receive it to ascend to Heaven.

His clearness of style, moreover, was one of the Saint's greatest merits. It occurred to him sometimes to have to explain points of doctrine that were most abstruse and far removed beyond the ordinary intelligence, yet he did it with such a happy choice of words that they who listened to him marveled at finding that they understood in its naked sense what before appeared to surpass their intellectual capacity. An admirable appropriateness reigned in his expressions; they were elevated or simple to suit the understanding of his hearers. By this means, he pleased the educated and instructed the ignorant. When he addressed himself to the poor people, his language was wonderfully adapted to their turn of mind. He generally cited for their interest facts from the lives of the Saints or from the Fathers; in this way he secured their attention, while he also confirmed his own words by the authority of example. He would sometimes relate to them what he himself had witnessed and what he had done; and as it was impossible to doubt his testimony, he never brought himself on the scene without exciting their interest to the highest pitch.

He usually chose for his subject the Last Judgment, and the practical conclusions which he drew therefrom were repentance, the reformation of conduct and a new life. One point on which he strongly insisted was the love of enemies. At that period, hereditary hatreds not infrequently armed whole cities and families against each other, which oftentimes resulted in cruel death. St. Vincent would not believe that he had done anything until he had publicly reconciled those whom enmity divided. His sermons were sometimes prolonged to an unusual length, for he would interrupt himself to give vent to the sighs and lamentations which his impassioned eloquence elicited from his audience. He paused at times himself to weep, and to calm his emotions; at other times it was to foretell some event or to work a miracle. In a word, these interruptions were often caused by his ecstasies, and when the rapture had ceased, he would take up the thread of his discourse as if nothing had occurred.

Such was St. Vincent Ferrer when in the pulpit.[2]

Chapter 7

The Company which Followed St. Vincent Ferrer
in the Course of His Miraculous Apostolate—
Extraordinary Fruits Produced by the Saint in
Pious Souls during that Period.

MOVED by the miracles of Our Lord and desirous to hear His doctrine, a great multitude followed His footsteps in traversing Judea and Samaria, where He went to preach the Kingdom of God. It was a feeling like this that drew around St. Vincent Ferrer certain persons, happy to follow him and to walk under his guidance in the path of salvation. The Saint felt it his duty to allow those persons to attach themselves to him. Their numbers failed not to increase, such that, in the course of time, there were thousands of devout pilgrims who associated themselves with him in his apostolic journeys.

But as all those who formed the retinue of Our Lord in the days of His public life were not attached to His Divine Person in the same degree (for there was at first the Apostolic College, composed of twelve members; then the disciples to the number of seventy-two, along with the holy women, who were not less devoted to the Son of God; and, finally, the rest of the multitude). Similarly, the followers of our Saint comprised three principal categories: the first consisted of religious of the Order of St. Dominic, seldom less than twelve; the second was composed of Tertiaries belonging to the same Order; and the third embraced a host of penitents, whose numbers sometimes swelled to the enormous figure of ten thousand.

The first class, which responded so exactly to the College of the Apostles, was a sort of movable convent, with their holy master at their head. These religious formed, as it were, a system of spiritual stars, of which he was the center and which revolved with him around the earth, shedding floods of light and warmth, making the flowers to blossom and the fruits to ripen for eternal life. To this first division were added many religious of various Orders who had obtained permission from their Superiors and from the Holy See to accompany the Saint. There were also those of the secular clergy. The whole numbered about fifty coadjutors, whose learning and solid virtues were usefully employed for the salvation of souls. These priests and religious supplied the Saint's place both in the pulpit and the confessional when he was ill; they also assisted him in administering the Sacrament of Penance to the people whom he converted. Moreover, to each one was given the sort of employment for which he was best suited. One wrote the letters, another catechised; this one was charged with the reconciliation of enemies, that one with the direction of the pilgrims. A treasurer was also appointed to receive the alms of the faithful, with which he provided for the wants of the company, and the rest he distributed among the poor.

The second class, which consisted of large numbers of persons of both sexes whom he had clothed with the habit of the Third Order of St. Dominic—with the sanction of the Holy See and the Superiors of the Order—were similar to Our Lord's seventy-two disciples and the holy women. The third comprised the other laity, both men and women, and represented the rest of the multitude who followed our Lord. Like the pilgrims of that period, all were clad in somber garments as a sign of repentance and humility. They were arranged in two distinct bands, male and female, and maintained that order at all times, both during the missions and on their journey. They traveled on foot and with staves in their hands. The men were preceded by a picture of the Crucifixion, the women by a banner of the Blessed Virgin. The religious and secular clergy, separated from the laity, grouped themselves around the Saint. Their march was announced by the ringing of a bell, the same that gave the signal for the working of miracles. St. Vincent also took with him notaries public, whose duty it was to draw up forms of agreement between enemies whom he reconciled.

As soon as they entered a city, which was always done with perfect recollection and becoming order, the men charged to provide for the material wants of the company sought out the families who were willing to receive one or more of the pilgrims; then they conducted the latter to the house where they were to receive hospitality. They applied only to ladies of irreproachable character. Generally speaking, the directors of the company in seeking lodgings for the pilgrims were embarrassed by the number of choices: The people contended who should afford them shelter, for their edifying life seemed to bring a blessing on the house which received them. The pilgrims paid all their own expenses, but frequently their hosts would refuse to receive anything from them, esteeming themselves abundantly recompensed by their good example and holy conversation.

Indeed, the heroic virtues practiced by these devout pilgrims was a sight which spoke to the eye with as much unction and eloquence as the sermons of the Saint did to the ear, for it embraced both the precept and example of Christian piety. This numerous staff surrounding St. Vincent accelerated the religious movement in the hearts of people which he inaugurated. Some instructed the ignorant; others gave to each one in particular the counsel which St. Vincent gave to all in general. They incited all to a prompt imitation of their example, and they imparted to the great exercises of Religion a pomp and enthusiasm which gradually won the heart by its salutary touch.

The Saint prescribed wise regulations both for the admission of the Faithful into this holy company and for their manner of life. Persons of doubtful reputation were rejected. Public sinners were required to have performed beforehand the most rigorous public penance and that they should still form a section apart from the rest and be called *Disciplinants*. Among these were to be found many who had once been notorious sinners, but who now expiated their crimes by edifying austerities. Confession and Communion were customary, at least once a week. This double practice contributed in uniting hearts to God by the closest ties and in binding together the members of society with the cords of Christian charity.

This numerous band, ten thousand in all, was composed of persons of every rank in life—the noble and the plebeian, the learned and the ignorant, priests and people of different nationalities, of different tastes and of different temperaments. Yet there reigned among them such perfect peace and charity that they exhibited to the world a faithful picture of the primitive Church. It might have been said of them that they had but one heart and one soul. The example of St. Vincent bound together this great brotherhood; the great supported the little with admirable patience; whereas the latter requited their condescension by their profound respect. The heads of the different divisions of the community put aside their own individual interests and had but one desire—the well-being of all.[1]

The wonderful preaching of the Saint produced immense fruit in the world, both among the good and the wicked. The one became more holy, the other were converted. When St. Vincent died, the state of souls in the Church had undergone a complete transformation.

Among the virtuous souls whom our Saint led to the summit of perfection we may cite, in the first place, the companions and coadjutors of his apostolate. The principal were:

1. Blessed Antony Fuster, of our Order. This man had a remarkable talent for appeasing enmities. St. Vincent having preached at Vich, in Catalonia, to a population torn by faction, left this Father there, who happily terminated the work begun by himself. Blessed Antony compelled the inhabitants of that town to renounce their projects of vengeance, and he united in mutual affection

those whom anger separated. Shortly after this general reconciliation, he went to receive in Heaven the reward of his apostolic labors.

2. Blessed Geoffrey of Blanes, of the same Order. This blessed Father was possessed of great eloquence. Many Bishops and Archbishops, in order to attract the faithful to his fruitful preaching, accorded various indulgences to those who should assist at his sermons or his Mass. History exhibits him as having a tender devotion to the Blessed Virgin Mary, who frequently appeared to him. In life, and after death, he wrought a great number of miracles. He died at Barcelona in the year 1414.

3. Blessed Peter Cerdan, also of the Order of Friar Preachers. When he joined the company of the Saint, he was simple and illiterate. But when his spiritual master died, he seemed to have inherited his eloquence. He preached with such talent and animation that he astonished all those who knew him. He died in 1422, in the city of Graus, in Catalonia. At the moment when he expired on his bed of vine-branches, his usual couch, the bells began to ring of themselves, and a heavenly light surrounded his sacred remains. His body was carefully kept, and several solemn translations of it took place. He was always honored with public veneration in the church of his Order, and the cures of many sick persons are attributed to his intercession.

4. Blessed Blase of Auvergne, who generously renounced his rich patrimony to enter the Order of Friar Preachers. He made great progress in virtue under the guidance of our Saint. God even favored him with great miracles. He died after the canonization of his master. His relics were preserved in the Convent of Sisteron, in Provence, where the veneration of the Saints has always been rendered to him.

5. Blessed Peter Quéralt, another Dominican. He shone with great glory in the company of St. Vincent. His life was prolonged till the year 1462. His body, having been buried in the Convent of Lerida, in Spain, remained entire until the wars of 1708, when it was cut in pieces by the soldiers.

6. Blessed John of Alcoy and Peter of Maya, also of the Order. They were the first to join St. Vincent Ferrer. Thus they were his most dear disciples. They replaced him when he was ill; they were penetrated with his spirit, excelled in preaching and both rose to the highest degree of sanctity.

7. The Ven. John of Gentilpré. He studied at Toulouse in 1417, when, won by the Saint's preaching, he, with two others, took the habit of the Friar Preachers and joined his company. He asked of God the grace to preach daily, and to die preaching. On the day of his death, the religious and several seculars surrounded his bed; he summoned all his strength, spoke to them of the King-

dom of God and died in the middle of this last exhortation.

8. The Ven. Martin of Vargas, a Cistercian, the reformer of the Convent of Piétra, and of most of the monasteries of his order in Spain.

9. Blessed John Gilabert, of the Order of Mercy. Obedience to the Saint's command caused him to leave his company. On arriving at the gate of the monastery to which he was assigned, he gave up his soul. His death was revealed to St. Vincent, who offered the Holy Sacrifice for him and preached a panegyric on his virtues.

What especially merits our attention is that a great number of those who piously followed the Saint in his apostolic journeys entered the Order of Friar Preachers or other religious Orders. Abandoning the world and their riches for the love of God, they peopled the monasteries of men and women. Schools and families suffered from these multiplied vocations. The impulse was universal—all desired to enter the cloister.

St. Vincent did not neglect the religious communities in the course of his apostolate. After his public discourses, he preached to the religious of monasteries. It would be impossible to describe his zeal for regular observance and the perfection of their state. Every time that he returned to Valencia, for example, he never failed to visit the Convent of the Sisters of St. Dominic, where he had a great number of spiritual daughters, and each time he animated them by his discourses to redouble their fervor in the service of God.

We shall crown this chapter with the names of four illustrious personages whom St. Vincent Ferrer inspired with a distaste for the world and with the love of God, and who, embracing the perfect life in the cloister, sanctified themselves therein. The first is the Saint's brother, Blessed Boniface Ferrer, who after becoming a widower, entered by his advice the Order of the Chartreux [the Carthusians]; he merited by his virtues to be elected General of the Order and was esteemed a Saint. Then there is St. Bernardine of Siena, whom in an interview St. Vincent advised to join the Order of St. Francis and whose future success in regard to souls he publicly foretold. There is also Blessed Margarite, Princess of Savoy, whom the Saint received into the Third Order of St. Dominic and whose sanctity has been recognized by the Church. And lastly, there was Blessed Agnes of Moncada, a poor florist, whom one of his sermons determined to vow perpetual virginity to God and who, following a special inspiration, like Magdalen retired to an unknown grotto, where after her death God manifested her sanctity by striking prodigies.[2]

Chapter 8

The Universal Conversion which the
Miraculous Apostolate of St. Vincent Ferrer
Produced in the Church—Its Abundant Fruits
Among Heretics and Jews.

———————

GOD alone knows the number of souls whom
our Saint led from sin to penance by a daily
course of preaching, extending over a period of
twenty years. But if we may judge by the exterior
signs which everywhere accompanied his presence, we can easily conceive that there would be
very few persons who were privileged to see and
to hear him and who could still resist the efficacy
of his influence on their souls.

And how was it possible to remain insensible to
his touch? He preached with such energy, such
vivacity and vigor, that he no longer appeared an
old man broken down by age and infirmity, but a
youthful herald of the Gospel, fired with an
impetuous ardor. He could be heard at a great distance around, and he was understood by people of
every nation, although he spoke only the Valencian dialect. His sudden display of energy during

his preaching was as a miracle which enraptured his hearers. On leaving the pulpit, he once again became feeble, weary and infirm; his countenance was pale, his walk slow, and he had need of the assistance of someone to support his steps. No one would have supposed him to be the same individual, nor could it be doubted that the Holy Spirit worked in him during his discourse to reanimate his enfeebled body and to produce in him this marvelous energy.

Another cause of success was the gift of miracles which he possessed in a rare degree. They were of daily occurrence. Wherever he went, he restored health to a great number of sufferers whose bodily cure was despaired of. We may well imagine, then, the impression which this wonderful spectacle so often repeated would everywhere produce. He moved rapidly from place to place, so great was his eagerness to evangelize the whole of Europe, but the prodigies which he daily accomplished left indelible traces in the hearts of all. The procession of *Disciplinants* was, moreover, capable in itself of softening the most hardened souls. It took place every evening at sunset, notwithstanding the state of the weather, in rain, snow, wind and tempest. It consisted of persons of every condition, the nobility and the common people, great and small, even children from four to five years old who were not afraid to scourge themselves in order to expiate the sins of the people. They walked two and two with naked feet, their faces veiled, clad in sackcloth and their shoulders bared in such a manner as not to offend against modesty. Each penitent scourged himself with a discipline, meditating on the Passion of our Lord. Their blood flowed, and carried away by the impetuosity of their fervor, some even went so far as to cut their flesh in pieces by the violence of the blows. And yet, strange as it may appear, none of these austere penitents ever suffered in their health at the close of this exercise. The Saint himself alluded to it, in order to show how agreeable to God was this sensible display of penance; in the space of twelve years, not a single death occurred among those who formed the special company of *Disciplinants.*

One day, while this procession traversed the streets of a city, women of disreputable character assembled in the church, and one of St. Vincent's companions preached to them on sin, repentance and Hell. Few of these unhappy women resisted the pressing exhortations that were addressed to them. They were seen on the following day to break asunder the ties which bound them to vice and to take part in the procession of public penance.

What was the result of all this? Exactly this— that from the moment of St. Vincent's entry into a city, it immediately wore the appearance of Nineve when Jonas preached penance to it. People wept when they heard the Saint's Mass, but their tears were most abundant when he exhorted them to repentance. It was then that sighs, groanings and lamentations filled the air. It might have been thought that each one mourned the death of a firstborn, or of a father or a mother. The squares and the plains which were covered by his listeners gave an idea of the Universal Judgment: It was, in fact, like the future terror and lamentation of all the tribes of the earth gathered together in the valley of Josaphat. But as Nicholas de Clémangis, an eyewitness, observes, the most lukewarm souls and hearts of stone were softened and gave vent to their sorrow in tears and accents of the bitterest anguish.

We may, moreover, picture to ourselves the extraordinary confluence of people. The Saint's audience was not composed solely of the inhabitants of the city where he preached. There were frequently gathered around his pulpit more than fifty thousand people, even when he preached in small villages. They gladly came several leagues to hear him [A league is approximately three miles]. During his sermon, all the artisans abandoned their labor and the merchants their warehouses. In cities where there were schools, the masters suspended their lectures. Neither the inclement season, wind nor rain, prevented the multitudes from collecting in the public squares where the Saint was to preach. The sick who had sufficient strength to walk left the hospitals; others were carried; all hoped that their bodies, as well as their souls would be cured at the same time, and this hope was frequently realized.

We may form from the following fact some idea of the eagerness with which he inspired the people to penance: Wherever St. Vincent went, the squares and other public places were invaded by peddlers whose commerce consisted solely in disciplines, hair-cloth, iron chains, sackcloth and other instruments of mortification.

There are related in the *Spiritual Instructions* many interesting examples of great sinners converted. As to the general fruits of his apostolate, we will quote from an authentic document, a letter written by the Council of Orihuela to the Bishop of Carthagena, in Spain: "The arrival of Vincent Ferrer has produced immense good in this country; it has been a grand occasion of salvation to all the Faithful. This city in particular, at the close of his preaching and by God's grace, is delivered from every vice and public sin. There is no one, great or small, who dares to swear by the Holy Name of God, the Blessed Virgin and the Saints, or to utter any other oath. Cards and dice are abolished. . . . No one ventures to conjure, cast lots,

explain signs, or consult fortune-tellers and sor-
cerers. . . . All noisy entertainments have been
given up. . . . The people of this city have never
confessed so frequently as at the present moment;
the priests are insufficient to hear the Confessions
and give Communion. On Sundays and Feasts of
Obligation all . . . go to Mass with devotion such
as no one could believe, much less expect to witness. Before the arrival of Master Vincent, the
churches were large; now they are small. . . . There
no longer exists in this city either offences or ran-
cour or enmity against anyone, but each one spon-
taneously and for God's honor pardons the other.
We have counted more than one hundred twenty-
three reconciliations; sixty-six deaths and a host
of broken limbs have been pardoned. Now everyone lives in peace and concord.[1] In the great city
of Toulouse, all the women of abandoned character have renounced their disorders."[2]

In St. Vincent's time, heresy took refuge in the
high valleys of the Pyrenees and the Alps. These
were the strongholds of the Albigenses, Vaudois,
Cathari and the Paterini, who, compelled by the
united power of the Church and of the temporal
princes to quit the cities and plains, went forth to
find in those inaccessible retreats the fatal liberty
of error. St. Vincent's zeal led him to climb the
mountains that he might carry the torch of faith
among the unhappy people who inhabited them.

In the process of his canonization, it is related that, at the close of only one discourse at Perpignan, an incalculable number of heretics embraced the True Faith. This one fact alone gives us the measure of his success in the Pyrenees. As to the Alps, we are told that he traversed them in an almost incredibly short space of time. On the French descent he undertook the conversion of three valleys in the diocese of Embrun, where heresy and the corruption of morals had made the greatest ravages. Accompanied by his faithful band of *Disciplinants* and pious pilgrims, he penetrated into these valleys, till then rebellious to the Word of God. The Saint's renown and the fame of his miracles brought crowds of heretics to his sermons. A few days only sufficed to work a change in their hearts and to soften their obduracy. There were, however, many who viewed with bitter jealousy this general enthusiasm and sought to slay him. Three times they attempted to execute their wicked design, but three times also did the visible protection of God shield him from their malice. Despairing then of ridding themselves of the presence of the preacher, these deluded people came in their turn to hear his sermons. God's grace drew them there; they were more deeply moved than the rest, and in a short time they gave unequivocal signs of sincere conversion. Wicked customs and gross superstitions soon disappeared from those valleys; they embraced the True Faith and submitted with docility to the Church's discipline. The most criminal of them repaired so effectually the scandals it had given, that it ceased to be called Valpourrie[3] and was henceforth known only by the name of Valpure.

Most of the valleys on the Italian descent of the Alps were also inhabited by heretics, especially in the diocese of Turin. St. Vincent visited them in order, preaching in each of them the Catholic truth and attacking error with vigorous and irresistible energy. By the mercy of God, they each received the Divine Word with much ardor, piety and respect. The Saint's learning, his fervor and miracles opened the eyes of all. He observed that the chief cause of error and heresy was the total absence of preaching. He gathered from the inhabitants of the country that for thirty years no one had preached to them except Vaudois who came regularly among them twice a year. In the valley of Loferio, he reclaimed the Bishop of that poor erring flock; in that of Angrogne he destroyed the schools in which the ministers of error were educated; at Val-du-Pont he led the Cathari to renounce their abominations; at Val-de-Lanz he converted the descendants of the murderers of St. Peter Martyr. He discovered in the diocese of Geneva a gross and wide-spread error. It was customary to celebrate every year, on the day following Corpus Christi, a feast in honor of the Orient, and confraternities were established under the name of St. Orient.[4] No preacher dared to declaim against this monstrous error; the religious and the secular clergy were threatened either with death or the withdrawal of offerings and alms. But St. Vincent was above all such servile fear. He spoke freely against this abuse and effectually put a stop to it. He found matters in a still more lamentable state in the diocese of Lausanne, where the peasantry were accustomed to offer an idolatrous worship to the sun. He instructed them in the worship of God and put to flight all such superstitious practices.

St. Vincent's mission was not less fruitful among the Jews than among heretics. He converted an incalculable number of them. God seemed to have accorded him a special grace for the conversion of people who are proverbially hostile to the Christian name. There was at that period a population of Jews both numerous and powerful in Spain. The process of his canonization shows that in the space of thirteen months he converted twenty thousand in Castile alone; that in the year 1415, within six months, more than fifteen thousand were led to embrace the true faith in Aragon and Catalonia, and that on another occassion in the same country over thirty thousand were baptized at the close of his preaching. The historians of the sect do not hesitate to confirm these facts by their own testimony. In a work entitled *Juehasin*, it is related that in the year 1412, a Friar named Brother Vincent, having preached to the Jews, the latter renounced their law to a number of more than two hundred thousand.

The Saint had an ardent zeal and tender love for these unhappy wanderers. In the cities where he found them, he took care that a place should always be reserved for them, and after his exhortations he treated them with much consideration. These acts full of sweetness gained their hearts. The learning of the great preacher completed their conviction, and they presented themselves in a body to receive Holy Baptism. Thus, at Perpignan seventy families embraced the Christian faith. In other places whole synagogues abjured their errors. Their place of meeting was changed into a church. In Castile, they were so unanimously converted that none remained, and the Bishop of Palencia saw himself deprived of a large revenue, produced by a special impost on them. Among the Jews whom St. Vincent brought to the Divine Messias, many of them in their turn became the apostles of their co-religionists. Thus, one of them, who was afterward raised to the Episcopate, had the satisfaction of making forty thousand proselytes among his fellow countrymen.

Chapter 9

The Apostolic Success of St. Vincent Ferrer
Among the Followers of Mohammed—
The Principal Countries and Cities in which the
Saint Preached in the Course of
His Miraculous Apostolate.

———————

THE Mohammedans, like the Jews, were
spread throughout different parts of Spain. In
proportion as the noble-hearted Spaniards recovered possession of their provinces which had been
subjugated by the Saracen invasion, they re-estab-
lished Christianity in all its rights and favored by
every means in their power the conversion of the
followers of Mohammed who dwelt in the country.
There were many, however, who resisted this
influence. Like the Jews, they possessed of wealth
and industry. It was necessary, therefore, to deal
gently with them. St. Vincent labored wtih all his
might to reclaim them from their unclean errors.
He spared neither suffering nor fatigue to lead
them to the saving waters of Baptism. And to this
end, wherever he preached, he compelled the
Mohammedans, by the King's order, to be present

at his discourses, reserving for them, as in the case of the Jews, the most convenient places.

But why constrain such people to hear him, since the law of Mohammed especially forbids his disciples to listen to Christian sermons? "This," said the Saint, "is one of the wicked artifices of this Antichrist, by which he directly closes the door of salvation to his followers. The Divine Word is the first condition for the success of the Gospel. He who hears it is easily drawn as by a kind of necessity to embrace the Holy Faith, provided it be announced with becoming dignity."

The Saracen King of Granada, Mohammed Aben-Baha, moved by the renown of his miracles, was desirous to see St. Vincent and to afford him liberty to preach in his kingdom. He therefore sent ambassadors to him, as to a prince, who informed him that he would have unrestricted license to announce the Gospel throughout the kingdom of Granada. The Saint was then in the neighborhood of Genoa, in Italy. He forthwith set out on foot to Marseilles, where a vessel was placed at his service. A favorable wind soon brought him to the port of Andalusia. On the morning following his arrival at Granada, St. Vincent began a course of sermons in the presence of the King, his whole court and innumerable people. The Mohammedans, unaccustomed to hear discourses addressed to a great multitude, were filled with astonishment and admiration. Such was the effect of his preaching that, after three sermons, eighteen thousand Moors were converted to the Christian Faith. St. Vincent promised himself an abundant harvest in this new field of labor, but the enemy of mankind sought to stifle its growth by sowing therein the seeds of discord. Aben-Baha himself, with his whole court, had resolved to receive Baptism, but the chiefs of the Mussulman superstition—determining at any cost to impede so great a good—menaced him with revolt, civil war and the subversion of his throne. "If you embrace the Gospel," said they, "your subjects who believe in the Koran will never consent to be ruled by a prince who has abjured the law of Mohammed to become a Christian." Aben-Baha feared to lose a perishable crown of the earth. Dismayed by the threats of those fanatics, he called St. Vincent to him and bade him depart from his kingdom, assuring him of his own personal esteem of him. "Return," said he, "into the countries of the Christians, and do so speedily, lest you oblige me to have recourse to violent measures against you. I should do it with regret, but I cannot allow you to remain." The Saint would gladly have exposed himself to persecution and death—the thought of martyrdom filled him with joy—but he was unwilling to excite the anger of the Mussulmen against the new converts or to expose them to the danger of apostasy.

He therefore left the kingdom of Granada, beseeching God to destroy in that country the reign of the crescent and to establish in its stead that of the glorious Cross. A century later the desires of the Saint were accomplished. Granada was in its turn conquered, and the barbarous Mussulman was driven back to the shores of Africa. We may not unreasonably suppose that the band of converts formed by our Saint increased as years rolled by, and that when the missionaries of the Gospel arrived in that country, they found the hearts of its people better disposed to embrace the great truths of Christianity.

St. Vincent's zeal did not slacken in consequence of these accidents. Some time later, when an opportunity occurred to him, he resolved to go into Africa to preach to the people of Mauritania and to the Arabs of the desert, but circumstances independent of his own will interfered with the accomplishment of this grand project. He, however, indemnified himself by laboring with renewed ardor for the conversion of the Mussulmen who were established in Christian countries. Ranzano, one of the Saint's biographers, relates that eighty thousand of those infidels were brought to the True Faith. This is a high figure and far exceeds the number given by Father Teoli, whose account appears to be more reliable, since in comparing the number of Jewish conversions with that of the Mohammedans, the latter is found to be considerably less.

But to resume the thread of our narrative, St. Vincent was truly another St. Paul, sent by God to bring back to the Faith of Christ a multitude of Jews and Mohammedans, to convert innumerable sinners and to harmonize the faithful of every nation and condition of life in the most perfect bonds of Christian fellowship. We are thus able to see at a glance the general effect of the miraculous apostolate which he received from Christ Himself at Avignon. The Saint was not afraid to affirm it with his own lips. In one of his sermons which he preached in Castile, in the year 1411, we read thus: "The End of the World cannot be far distant, and the kingdom of God is at hand. Has not our Lord Himself said that the bearing of the fig-tree foreshadows the coming summer? Behold, then, the fig-tree of the Christian people. Each day records its reconciliations, and we witness souls forgetting and forgiving the greatest injuries. The delicate, the sensual and the vicious do penance. Obstinate sinners are converted and frequently approach the Sacraments. Nor is the Jewish fig-tree any longer barren, for we see it daily producing its abundant and choicest fruits in every city in Spain." He might have added heretics and

Mussulmen likewise. Truly, then, St. Vincent exercised in the Church an apostolate such as never was witnessed since the establishment of the Gospel.[1]

St. Vincent having evangelized Avignon and the neighboring towns, set out on foot for Spain, preaching in various places where he was obliged to stay.

It was at Graus, in Catalonia, that he instituted the procession of *Disciplinants* and laid the foundation of that marvelous company of pious souls who accompanied him in his apostolic journeyings. Here also he left behind him, as a souvenir, a crucifix which the inhabitants begged of him, and which became the instrument of many miracles.

From Graus, the Saint went to Barcelona, a city which he frequently visited and where he was always received with extraordinary respect. On one of these visits he beheld the Guardian Angel of the city, and on his relating the occurrence to the inhabitants, they constructed near the gate where he had this vision, a chapel dedicated to this heavenly protector.

While at Cerveva, St. Dominic appeared to Vincent in his cell, to encourage him in the execution of Our Lord's commands. The Saint preached everywhere with extraordinary success, God's confirming his words by striking prodigies.

In the beginning of the year 1400, our illustrious preacher left Catalonia and following the southern coast of France, arrived in Provence. Aix and Marseilles heard his voice. He announced in like manner the good news of salvation in many small towns and villages; and that no one might be deprived of it, he sent priests of his company into the places where he himself could not go.

Having preached the Lent of 1402 at Marseilles, Vincent went to the Romans for an interview with Father John de Puynoix, General of the Order, to lay before him the plans of his mission and to solicit his paternal blessing. The Father General sanctioned his proceedings, exhorted him to pursue his vocation till death and lovingly blessed so worthy a subject.

It was then that Vincent journeyed into the valleys of the diocese of Embrun and entirely transformed them. He passed from thence, from the side of the Alps, into Piedmont and Lombardy and then into the state of Genoa. In 1403, he was in the Marquisate of Montferrat. Crossing again the Alps, he was at the close of that year at Chambray, where he founded a convent of Friars of his Order. In 1404, he preached the Lent at Lausanne. Toward the end of August, he left Switzerland. On the 6th of September he was at Lyons, where he preached for 14 days with extraordinary results. After traversing the whole of Lyonnais, St. Vincent arrived in Lorraine, and passed from thence into Flanders.

While preaching in the latter country, Benedict XIII enjoined him to accompany him to Genoa, where he was to hold a conference with the Italian Cardinals, with reference to putting an end to the schism. Vincent obeyed his orders. But learning on the route that the journey to Genoa was deferred till the spring of 1405, he stayed at Auvergne. The city of Claremont heard his exhortations during Advent and Lent.

In the month of May, 1405, he was at Genoa with Benedict XIII. There he beheld with sorrow every effort that was made to extinguish the schism rendered abortive. Nothing remained to him then but to evangelize the population, and he traversed the coast of the state of Genoa. At Savone, he received an embassy of the Mussulman King of Granada, who invited him to preach the Kingdom of God in his capital. We have already related how he yielded to this request, the extraordinary success of his preaching among the Mohammedans, the jealousy of the chiefs of this false religion and the obligation he was under of abandoning a harvest already so ripe. These events occurred in the year 1406.

On leaving Granada, St. Vincent pursued his apostolic missions in Andalusia. The whole city of Baéza was converted by his preaching; and Ezija and Seville profited not less thereby.

From there he passed into Castile. Here he

received letters and ambassadors from Henry IV,
King of England, who entreated him to come into
Great Britain to evangelize its people. St. Vincent,
whose charity would willingly have embraced the
whole world, joyfully accepted the King's proposal, and arriving at San Sebastian, a port in the
Gulf of Gascony, he was conveyed to England in a
vessel sent expressly to bring him. He arrived in
the summer of the year 1406. The indefatigable
apostle remained over a year in these islands,
preaching throughout the kingdom and producing
the same results as in his other missions. Having
thus evangelized England, Scotland and Ireland,
he returned into France toward the Autumn of
1407.

He would doubtless travel by sea to Bordeaux,
since historians speak of him as passing from
England into Gascony. He went from there into
Picardy and Poitou. In 1408, he preached during
Lent in Auvergne; then he crossed the Pyrenees to
preach once more throughout Spain. A record of
that period shows that he journeyed from one
country to another on horseback. He had then a
wound in the leg which tortured him during the
last eleven years of his life. Yet his sufferings in no
way hindered him from pursuing his apostolate;
the happiness of laboring for the salvation of souls
made him forgetful of suffering. Having passed
through the north of Spain—where in Cuença and

Molina he was pained at witnessing the barren effects of his preaching—he arrived at Perpignan, where Benedict XIII had convoked a council. The obstinacy of Peter de Luna [Benedict XIII] paralyzed the good results of that assembly. Grieved at the unhappy dispositions of the Pontiff, Vincent resumed the course of his preaching till he reached Montpellier, and after a fruitful mission, he returned once more to Perpignan. There he received letters from the King of Aragon, dated the 22nd of January, 1409, who called him to Barcelona to confer with him on business of importance.

In obeying the summons of that prince, Vincent availed himself of the opportunities which the journey afforded him to preach at Elne, Girone and Vich. When he arrived at Barcelona in the month of June, 1409, he was not content with attending the King in council, but continued his apostolic preaching, which produced marvelous fruits. Toward the end of the same year, a vessel conveyed him into Tuscany. He traveled through the dioceses of Pisa, Lucca, Florence and Siena, everywhere converting sinners and reviving Christian piety. At the commencement of the year 1410, he returned to Barcelona and traversed once more the whole of Catalonia and Aragon. It was at this epoch that he instituted a university at Valencia, his native city. He came from there into Castile. At Salamanca he raised a woman to life, to prove to his audience that he was himself the Angel Precursor of the Judgment, announced in the Apocalypse. [*Apoc.* 14:6]. This miracle is related in detail in the *Spiritual Instruction* for the fifth Friday before the Saint's Feast. The succession to the throne of King James of Aragon, who died childless, led him to return to Barcelona. He was constrained to occupy himself with this affair, and after many negotiations, full of patience and wisdom, he turned it to the advantage of his country. In 1413, St. Vincent evangelized the Balearic Isles. In 1414, he went to Tortosa, where he converted many Jews. Then he returned to Saragossa, and remained there till the beginning of the year 1415, preaching with much fruit. He was a second time drawn by the Spirit of God toward central Italy, and so great was the success of his apostolate, especially in Bologna, that its inhabitants were pleased to accord him the title of citizen. Returning from there into Spain, he was speedily summoned to the Congress of Perpignan, in which the obstinacy of Peter de Luna showed itself more strongly than ever. St. Vincent was so deeply afflicted that he fell grievously ill. The glorious confessor, refusing medical succor, placed his entire confidence in Our Lord. Jesus Christ appeared to him, consoled him, cured him and announced to him that he should yet visit other countries.

The Congress of Perpignan was fatal to Peter de Luna. Through the advice of the theologians, and of St. Vincent in particular, the King of Aragon detached himself from his obedience to Benedict XIII, and from that moment the cause of the union was accomplished.

The King's edict was published on the 6th of January, 1416.[2]

Our Saint spent the beginning of the year in traveling through many provinces of Aragon to withdraw the people from obedience to Benedict XIII, and to attach them to that of the Council of Constance, an undertaking by no means easy considering the long period in which those countries had lived under the spiritual dominion of Peter de Luna. But to all their prejudices the Saint opposed solid reasons, which carried conviction to every mind. In a short time, Spain, as well as Italy and the rest of Christendom, awaited with submission the choice of the Council of Constance, ready to acknowledge the elect of the Council as the veritable Vicar of Jesus Christ.

The King of Aragon, well knowing how advantageous to the interests of the Church would be the presence of St. Vincent, entreated him to go to Constance as his theologian. But the latter declined this honor, believing it was better to follow the extraordinary mission which God had confided to him. He then went into Languedoc. At

the end of January, 1416, history points to him at
Carcassone. From there he went to Bésziers and
Montpellier; then, retracing his steps, he preached
throughout Roussillon. In the month of March,
Vincent passed again into the diocese of Carcas-
sonne, and that year he celebrated the festival of
the Annunciation at Montolieu, where he wrought
the miraculous cure recorded in the *Spiritual
Instruction* for the first Friday preceding the
Saint's Feast.

From Montolieu, Vincent journeyed onward to
Toulouse. Two Fathers of his Order awaited him at
Castanet. He entered the city on the Friday before
Palm Sunday, amid pompous solemnities, and was
received as an angel from Heaven. In the evening
of his arrival, a procession of public penance took
place. The number of those who took part in it was
extraordinary. Besides the grown-up people, there
were three hundred little children who scourged
their tender shoulders with the discipline.

We may judge by these prognostications of the
immense good which the preaching of St. Vincent
Ferrer would produce in Toulouse. There especially were realized the marvelous fruits of which
we have given but a feeble description in the seventh chapter of this Section. The sermons lasted a
month, but their results were as abundant as
though the Saint had preached a whole year. The
priests of the city, and the religious who accompa-

nied Vincent in his missions, hardly sufficed to receive the Confessions of those that were converted. They who had enriched themselves by fraud and injustice restored their ill-gotten gains; they who had long scandalized the city by the openness of their crimes were desirous to edify it by public repentance. The penances that were imposed on these great sinners did not seem to them sufficient, but they believed themselves bound to the severest expiation. All the women of ill-fame abandoned their disorders and gave unequivocal and consoling proofs of the sincerity of their conversion.

The Saint left behind him in the city the greater part of the pious women who had followed him till then. They dwelt together in community and observed the rules which he gave them.

On the 3rd of May, Vincent left Toulouse. He was accompanied as far as Portet, where he gave a short mission and then went on to Muret. Having held a station in that town, he passed into the district of Caraman. From there he journeyed to Saïx and Castres. In the latter city, he received an express invitation from the Fathers of the Council of Constance to join them, the invitation being transmitted to him by an emissary of the King of Aragon. When this was notified to him, he started in the direction of the city where the Council was sitting, but traveled by short stages in order to preach to the people whom he might encounter on the journey.

He reached Alby on the 28th of May, 1416, and preached there eight days. Then traversing the country, he visited Gaillac, Cordes and Najac and arrived on the 22nd of June at Villefranche du Rouergne, where he gave a mission that lasted five days. After that he went to Rodez. Tradition says he preached in a large meadow of the Priory of St. Felix, which is not far distant. He passed from there across the mountains of Auvergne to reach by a direct route Puy-en-Véley. In the latter city he found an ambassador of John VI, Duke of Brittany, who invited him into his dominions. The Saint promised to respond to the wishes of the prince, but was desirous first to journey to Constance and to preach in the neighboring provinces on the German frontier. He traversed the eastern portion of Auvergne and Bourbonnais and then entered the Duchy of Bourgogne.

At Dijon, St. Vincent received a solemn embassy of the Council of Constance with a Cardinal at its head. Certain difficulties of grave importance were proposed to him, which the man of God explained with such wonderful lucidity that the ambassadors marveled at the clearness and solidity of his judgment. When the Fathers of the Council were apprised of the Saint's answer, they shared the admiration of their envoys and accepted it as an oracle. History does not inform us of the nature of the questions at issue, nor of the solution given thereto. But when the ambassadors withdrew, instead of pursuing his journey to Constance, Vincent directed his steps toward Brittany, either because he had been dispensed from attending the Council, or because he no longer considered his presence necessary after the answer he had given to the questions which had been submitted to him.

Leaving Dijon, he passed through Champagne. At the celebrated Monastery of Clairvaux, he cured the pestilential fevers with which the community were afflicted. Langres and many other cities of that province enjoyed the privilege of seeing and hearing him. He pushed on his course as far as Nancy, the capital of Lorraine, where he again received an embassy of the Duke of Brittany, who implored him to hasten into his dominions. The Saint, considering himself bound to yield to such pressing solicitations, left Lorraine and traveled toward Brittany by way of Berry. The Archbishop of Bourges had conceived certain unfavorable impressions of him, which disappeared as soon as he had seen and heard him, and from that moment he manifested the greatest goodwill toward him. Crossing Berry into Lorraine, St. Vincent converted its capital, which was a Babylon of iniquity, into a Jerusalem of peace and virtue.

There a third messenger from the Duke of Brittany rejoined him. He then hastened his journey to that country through Anjou. Preaching at Angers against the excessive extravagance of the women, he effectually put a stop to the scandal.

It was in the beginning of March, 1417, that St. Vincent entered Brittany, where, two years later, he was to terminate his career.[3]

Chapter 10

The Saint's Last Apostolic Journeys in
Brittany—To the Council of Constance—
In Normandy—and Again in Brittany.

THE first city in Brittany which St. Vincent
evangelized was Nantes. There he preached
morning and night the twelve days following and
wrought so many conversions and miracles that
the inhabitants declared they had never before witnessed anything like it. This city was steeped in
every type of crime, but at the close of the mission
it was completely changed; religion was deeply
planted therein and practiced, and the morals of its
people became holy and pure.

From Nantes, the Saint proceeded to Vannes,
where the Duke and Duchess of Brittany resided.
They gave him a reception which equalled, if it
did not surpass, that which was accorded him at
Toulouse. Many wealthy lords invited him to
lodge in their palaces, but he refused those sumptuous abodes and chose as his residence a humble
cottage belonging to a person named Robin
Scarb. His entry into Vannes took place on the

20th of March, the Saturday before the Fourth Sunday in Lent. The text of the opening discourse, which he preached on the following morning, was taken from the Gospel of the day: *Colligite quae superaverunt fragmenta*—"Gather up the fragments that remain." (*John* 6). These words, as would appear, bore a prophetic meaning; they invited the Bretons to profit by the last days of his preaching on earth, the last fragments of God's Word, which he had so long distributed to the multitude. The inhabitants of Vannes fully understood the Saint's appeal; all sinners were converted. While the mission lasted, the law-courts were vacated and the shops closed. The only occupation of all was to make their Confessions, to do penance, to repair the injustice done to their neighbors and to be reconciled to their enemies. So desirous were they to hear the Saint that neither the inclemency of the season nor the piercing cold nor the rain nor the snow which fell at that period, could deter the thousands of his listeners from pressing around the pulpit. We must not forget that St. Vincent always preached in the open air.

Among the graces which the Saint's prayers brought to the ducal family of Brittany may be singled out the blessing of parenthood, for we may justly attribute to the merit of his prayers the birth of Duke Peter, who in later times took an active part in the work and expenses of the Saint's canonization.

The Count de Rohan, having heard the renown of this new Apostle, conceived a lively desire to have him in his dominions. To satisfy his piety, St. Vincent went to Josselin, a small town in the diocese of St. Malo. He preached there for the space of eight days with the usual happy results. He then proceeded to Rennes, and from there to Dinan and Lamballe.

In the latter town our Saint received pressing letters from the illustrious Chancellor Gerson, one of the lights of the Council of Constance. That great man once more invited Vincent to come to the august assembly of the Universal Church, to aid it by his counsel and to edify it by his example. The learned Peter d' Ailly, Cardinal Archbishop of Cambray, having added a postscript to Gerson's letter, Vincent judged it fitting to yield to their request. He had, moreover, a particular interest in explaining and justifying his conduct before the Church. Whether through ignorance or from malice, there were many who confounded the sect of *Flagellants,* who arose at that epoch, with the *Disciplinants* of St. Vincent Ferrer. Gerson gave him prudent and charitable advice regarding this. It behooved him, he said, to contradict these false and injurious reports. St. Vincent then hastened on his way to Germany and reached Constance some days before the last session of the Council. His presence smoothed over the difficulties that yet remained. On the 11th of November, 1417, measures were able to be taken to proceed to the election of a Sovereign Pontiff, which ended in the nomination of Martin V. After this great achievement, St. Vincent delivered a discourse in Latin, to thank God for the re-establishment of union and peace in the Church.

Toward the close of the same year or at the commencement of the following, the holy Apostle, thinking that the election of the Sovereign Pontiff rendered his sojourn at Constance no longer necessary and desiring to continue his preaching among the people whom he had begun to evangelize, left Germany and hastened his return into Brittany. He spent the whole of the month of April, 1418, in traversing the province of Anjou, and gathering on every side most abundant fruits. Wishing afterwards to fulfill a promise he had made to the King of England, he proceeded into Normandy. He preached at St. Lô at Caen, where the King was staying, and in many other towns in the province, instructing the people throughout and reforming their morals.

In the meantime, the Duchess of Brittany informed the Saint that she was about to give birth to another child and requested him to come to baptize it immediately after its birth. St. Vincent obeyed the summons, preaching on his journey in the Dioceses of Rennes, St. Malo, St. Brieuc, Quimper and Nantes. Arriving in this last city toward the end of the month of November, he preached the Advent, and thence directed his steps to Vannes at the close of the year 1419.

He rested on the way at the Cistercian Abbey of Notre Dame des Prières. Here he was seized with a grievous malady, the first symptom of his approaching end. As soon as he could support the fatigues of traveling, without, however, being completely restored, he resumed his journey to Vannes, where he arrived at the end of February. He was received with indescribable enthusiasm. The Duchess would gladly have lodged him in her own palace, but the Saint once more repaired to the cottage of Robin Scarb.

Unmindful of his sufferings and fatigue, he began immediately to preach, but his bodily weakness soon betrayed itself, and he was compelled to succumb. He then exercised the sacred ministry in another way—he instructed the children in Christian doctrine, which, in the latter days of his life, was his most cherished occupation.

This brilliant star of the Church set at Vannes. Before, however, recounting the circumstance of his death, the glory with which God accompanied it and the devotion which has been paid to him, even to our own times, we may be permitted to give a feeble outline of some of the virtues of this great Saint and of the extraordinary gifts with which God favored him.

—SECTION FOUR—

THE VIRTUES OF ST. VINCENT FERRER.

Chapter 11

The Virtues of St. Vincent Ferrer in Relation
To the Service of God—The Saint's Charity
Toward His Neighbor—His Heroic Devotedness
To the Temporal Necessities of His Brethren.

———————

THE heart of our Saint was forever attached to God by the sweet bonds of faith, hope and love. We shall comprehend the liveliness of his faith by the vast number of miracles which he wrought from the beginning of his life to the day of his death. It is to faith that the Gospel attributes the accomplishment of marvels. "If you have faith as a grain of mustard seed," said our Lord, "you shall say to this mountain, Remove from hence hither, and it shall remove." (*Matt.* 17:19). The faith of St. Vincent was doubtless very great, since every day of his life, so to speak, was marked by the miracles which flowed therefrom.

We have already stated with what care he learned from his childhood the truths of religion. He inculcated them in others with equal solicitude. One of the occupations of his ministry, to which he attached special importance, was to

teach the ignorant and children the words and
meaning of the Apostles' Creed. He recommended
all to recite, morning and evening, this profession
of faith as a defensive weapon against error.
Moreover, he earnestly exhorted Christians to
conform their practice to their belief. "The dia-
mond," said he, "is easily lost in the dunghill, and
the precious pearl of faith is in great danger of
being lost in a conscience defiled with the filth of
sin."

The Saint's hope was even more lively. He made
daily use of the means of salvation instituted by
Divine Providence. He made his Confession every
day and received the Sacrament of the Eucharist;
he faithfully accomplished the duties of his calling, and he did not resist the inspirations of grace.
Few Saints have been favored to the same degree.
We allude especially to the assurance, which was
on many occasions divinely revealed to him, on
the subject of his eternal salvation and of his predestination to great glory.

But this sentiment was not confined to himself
alone; he felt it even in regard to others. We will
cite here another example: A sick person at the
hour of death fell into despair at the sight of the
crimes with which he felt his conscience bur-
dened. He refused to purify his soul by sacramental Confession, replying to the priests who
exhorted him to this act that his iniquities were too

great—the language of the unhappy Cain. The
Saint, who was then in the neighborhood, being
apprised of the dying man's condition and of the
evil dispositions which animated him, hastened to
him and spoke tenderly to him. But the latter
answered him as he had done the others, with
words of despair. St. Vincent replied: "You well
know, however, my dear brother, that the good
Jesus died for you on the cross; why then despair
of His mercy?" These words, instead of softening
the miserable man, only incited his fury, and in a
paroxysm of impiety he exclaimed: "It is precisely
on that account that I wish to be damned, to dis-
please Jesus Christ." The depth of this despair
excited further the hope of St. Vincent, who, full
of confidence in the mercy and omnipotence of
God, turned his face toward the dying man and
said: "I will save thee in spite of thyself." He
immediately invited those present to invoke with
fervor the Holy Virgin, mother of all goodness and
to recite the Rosary. God was pleased to show, by
a miraculous manifestation, how pleasing to Him
was the heroic hope of His servant. Before the
Rosary was at an end, the sick man's chamber was
flooded with an immense light, and the Mother of
God appeared. She bore in her arms the Divine
Child, who was covered with bleeding wounds.
The despairing sinner, witness of this spectacle,
was totally changed. Full of compunction, he

asked pardon of God and of man for the blasphemies which he had uttered, and having received the Sacraments of the Church, shortly afterwards he expired, with his soul prepared to ascend to Heaven.[1]

Another sign of his unbounded hope in God's Providence was the little solicitude which he evinced in the course of his great apostolate, either for his own personal maintenance or that of the numerous company which followed him. His confidence in his heavenly Father never failed him. Neither he nor his companions were ever in want, and on one occasion Our Lord came miraculously to their aid.

Who shall say how ardent was the love which consumed the heart of St. Vincent Ferrer for his God, his Creator, his Redeemer? He thought always of Him; he preserved a constant remembrance of His benefits; he glorified Him forever in the depths of his soul. His conversation, like that of his blessed Father St. Dominic, was all in God. This love of his frequently drew sighs from his heart and tears from his eyes.

What did he not do to procure God's glory and the extension of His Kingdom in souls? It was to consecrate himself entirely to this that he renounced the delights of solitude, traveled Europe through and through, crossed mountains and plains, suffered hunger and thirst, cold and heat and endured untold fatigue. How generously he despised the riches and honors of the world! He was sensitive only to what was offensive to God. Seeing the iniquities which covered the world in his day, he fell so grievously ill at Avignon and Perpignan, that he was in imminent danger of death. A heavenly hand restored him to health, which he entirely devoted to glorifying God and saving souls.

This idea of God's glory completely absorbed him, and reasonably supposing that the esteem of which he was the object among men and the honor which was paid to him referred to the Divine praise and not to himself, he yielded to them—not through feelings of vanity, but out of pure love of God. He willingly allowed his hands to be kissed and pieces of his habit to be divided among the people as relics. He knew by experience that such was indeed the will of God, and it was manifested in a remarkable manner to the whole of his native city. Going on one occasion to Valencia, and before entering the city, he sent some of his disciples to prepare the customary reception with the most pompous solemnity. But the Duke of Cordova, who that year resided at Valencia under the auspices of Viceroy, attributed this triumphant display to pride and declined to sanction it. Yet scarcely had he expressed his refusal, when all the bells in the city began to ring without any visible cause. The inhabitants understood the meaning of the prodigy, and of their own accord they went forth to meet their illustrious townsman with all the pomp and magnificence which they could command. The bells continued to sound forth their merry chimes until the Saint arrived at the convent of his Order.[2]

Shall we speak also of the tender devotion of St. Vincent toward the Blessed Virgin and the Saints? Preaching, as he was accustomed, at least twice a day, he did not allow a single day to pass without saying something about the Saint whose feast it was. He dwelt on their glory and virtues and inflamed all hearts with the desire to honor and imitate them. A young man of Barcelona, having heard him on the Feast of St. Margaret extol the triumphs of that young martyr over the devil, burned with the desire to rush into combat with the enemy of salvation. Meeting in the way a poor old man who was deaf and who uttered some inarticulate words, he took him for Satan, and falling furiously upon him, severely maltreated him. St. Vincent stayed the death of the poor man until he could receive the Sacraments with becoming dispositions, while he also rebuked the imprudence of the youth. This act, nevertheless, shows us the ardor which animated him for the glory of the Saints.

If faith and zeal for God's glory and the desire

to render his ministry efficacious induced St. Vincent Ferrer to work wonders, it behooves us to add that another motive also led him to beseech God to accomplish them: this was the tender compassion which he felt for the pains, sorrows and sufferings of men. Hence those sudden deliverances from inevitable danger, those cures of every type of malady, those resuscitations even from death, which he effected while living. When six years old, he was taken to a child of his own age, who was afflicted with a dangerous pustule in the neck. He was told to touch the affected part. Vincent was not content with touching the wound, he kissed it. From the moment that his lips came into contact with the purulent flesh, the malady was instantaneously cured, and the wound closed.[3]

We read how readily he cured a poor man at Montolieu who importuned him. He often forestalled the wishes of sufferers. Preaching one day at Lerida, in the presence of the King of Aragon and an immense multitude assembled in one of the public squares, he stopped in the midst of his discourse and exclaimed that he saw at the distance of half a league [approximately one and a half miles] a poor paralytic striving with the utmost difficulty to reach the city. He besought the King to despatch some of his servants to his aid and to bring him before him. Two persons went off immediately, and they found the afflicted man, who was making ineffectual efforts to proceed. They took him in their arms and brought him to the Saint. As they were approaching the platform on which he stood, raising his hand, he made the Sign of the Cross over the paralytic. At the same instant the sufferer was completely cured and ran to the Saint to thank him. To express still more his gratitude, he attached himself to the Saint for a long space of time.[4]

On another occasion, a woman came in deep desolation to see him. She had been unfaithful to her marriage vows during the prolonged absence of her husband and was on the point of disclosing her shame by an adulterous childbirth. To complete her misery, she received a letter from her husband announcing his speedy arrival. She then went to seek aid and counsel of the man of God. St. Vincent first exhorted her to repentance, then encouraged her to have confidence in God, and promised her that her husband's arrival should be delayed until there was no longer any danger. The event proved the truth of his words and the efficacy of his prayers. The husband put off his return for an indefinite time. The woman was wholly astonished at the delay, and in the interval was relieved of her embarrassment without compromising either her conscience or her reputation. When the husband at length arrived, the woman said to him: "You told me in your letter that you would speedily return; why then have you tarried so long?" The man replied: "I was returning not far from here when my mules, laden with goods, ran away. I was obliged to go after them and have spent many days in consequence. At length I found them, and thank God, none of the goods which they carried has been lost. The only injury that I have sustained is the loss of the few days during which I went in pursuit of them." The woman fully comprehended the providential reason for the accident; she was filled with thankfulness to God and to His servant; and she repaired also the injury she had done by leading thereafter an irreproachable life.[5] Thus did St. Vincent save a woman who was deserving of infamy and death, and possibly even of eternal damnation.

On another occasion he came to the aid of a woman who was unjustly accused by her husband. She gave birth to a child, and this man pretended, though he knew better, that the child was not his own. His intention was to separate himself from her, and he was desirous of having some apparent reason for doing so. Conscious only of her innocence, the unhappy mother, a prey to mortal anguish, went to confide her troubles to St. Vincent, who, she was informed, never refused consolation to the afflicted. The Saint indeed gave her great comfort and said to her, "Come to my next sermon, bid your husband mix with the audience,

and do not neglect to bring your baby with you."
The woman faithfully obeyed the instructions
given her. When St. Vincent had opened his discourse, he in the presence of a vast multitude
addressed himself to a little child only a few days
old: "Leave thy mother's arms," he said, "and go in
search of thy father in the midst of this great
crowd of people." Wonderful to relate! The little
child received in a miraculous manner the use of
its feet, and threaded its way through the assembly
of people unassisted, and seizing the hand of its
mother's husband, it cried out: "This is my father;
I am really his child!" The people were deeply
affected at the sight of this prodigy. The reprehen-
sible father, thus publicly convicted of his fault,
sobbed aloud, asked pardon of his wife for having
calumniated her and made full reparation for his
fault by the assiduous practice of every domestic
virtue.

We will cite, moreover, the following example
of our Saint's ardent charity. A woman near the
term of pregnancy who was in dread of suffering
sent for him and implored him to deliver her from
the agonies which threatened her at the moment
of childbirth. St. Vincent exhorted her to patience
and observed that the sufferings of that hour were
the effect of God's will and of a law which had
been in force since the beginning of the world.
"Doubtless so," replied she, redoubling her

importunities, "but He who made that law can, by a miracle, exempt me from it, and I hope He will do so by the merits of your blessing." Seeing her confidence, St. Vincent said to her, "Have courage, my good woman, I will take the burden on myself, and you shall not sustain any harm at that critical moment." He then blessed her and departed. The hour arrived, and St. Vincent felt within himself physical suffering equivalent to that of a woman in travail. As to the person who had sought his help, she experienced neither accident nor pain of any kind. Such is the charity of the Saints. They are not content with sharing the sufferings of their brethren, but joyfully take the whole on themselves. Thus the Seraphic Virgin of Siena took entirely on herself the pains of Purgatory which her father ought to have suffered; thus also did St. Michael-des-Saints of the Order of the Trinity, with God's permission, undertake a malignant fever from which a friend of his was suffering. The Great Model of Saints gave the first example of this. "Surely He hath borne our infirmities," says the prophet, "and carried our sorrows." (*Isaias* 53:4).[6]

St. Vincent left behind him lasting memorials of his admirable charity. The number of hospitals, asylums, refuges, churches and even bridges which he founded during his apostolic journeyings is almost incredible. Having at his disposal a considerable staff in the bands of people who accompanied him, he availed himself of their services to build hastily those edifices consecrated to charity. He left some of these in almost every country through which he passed. One of his most remarkable foundations was the orphanage at Valencia, his birthplace, an establishment which has borne his name even to this day.

St. Vincent de Paul gloried in St. Vincent Ferrer as his patron, and we can well conceive that the examples of charity in the model were not without their influence on the holy priest who tried to walk in his footsteps.

Portrait of St. Vincent Ferrer at Valencia. This is considered the most authentic existing portrait of the Saint. (*Picture from the books of Père Fages, O.P., Louvain, Paris.*)

St. Vincent Ferrer reconciling enemies. (*Picture from the books of Père Fages, O.P., Louvain, Paris.*)

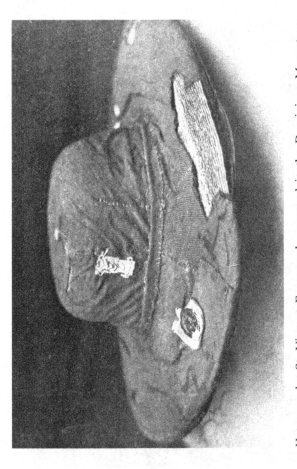

Hat worn by St. Vincent Ferrer and preserved in the Dominican Monastery, Lyons. *(Picture from the books of Père Fages, O.P., Louvain, Paris.)*

Photo: Maria Noel

Tomb of St. Vincent Ferrer in the Cathedral in Vannes.

Bust-reliquary of St. Vincent Ferrer containing (in the circle on the Saint's chest) part of his skull and lower jawbone. This bust is located just behind St. Vincent's tomb in the Cathedral in Vannes. (See facing page.)

Photo: Maria Noel

The house where St. Vincent Ferrer died: "Place Valencia," in Vannes, Brittany, France.

Chapel and Shrine of St. Vincent Ferrer in the Cathedral, Vannes. (*Picture from the books of Père Fages, O.P., Louvain, Paris.*)

Wooden half-length statue of the Saint at I'lle-aux-Moines,
a small island in the Gulf of Morbihan.

Statue of St. Vincent Ferrer at St. Dominic's Monastery at Dubruvnik, Croatia.

Statue of St. Vincent Ferrer at the Church of Santo Domingo
(St. Dominic) in Lima, Peru, which houses the tombs of St.
Martin de Porres, St. Rose of Lima and St. John Masias. The
baby in the statue represents a dying baby who was restored
to health by St. Vincent.

Chapter 12

Incomparable Zeal of St. Vincent Ferrer for the Salvation of Souls—Other Virtues of the Saint.

THE principal object of the Order of Friar Preachers is to labor for the salvation of souls. Thus did the Saint comprehend it, and to this end did he apply himself with such ardor. His constant study was to find out every means possible to withdraw souls from sin, to reconcile them to God and to conduct them in the paths of perfect sanctity.

While at Avignon, he was informed of an ecclesiastical dignitary whose life was not conformable to the holiness of his state. He spent the whole night in prayer to God for his conversion. At daybreak, being moved by a divine inspiration, he went to the prelate's palace with a crucifix in his hand, and entering, he pushed his way into the chamber where he reposed. He immediately opened one of the windows, and returning to the prelate, who was in bed, addressed him thus: "My son," said he, "behold the Divine Jesus, and consider how good and full of love He is! You fly from

Him, but He comes with confidence to the very
foot of your bed to find you. Make then your
peace, my son, make your peace with Jesus. What
does it avail you to have so often offended Him? It
is enough! It is enough! Embrace your sweet Master and love Him." Saying this, he placed the crucifix to the lips of the ecclesiastic and hastily left
him. The prelate, stupefied and ashamed, entered
into himself, and pressing the image of our Lord
to his breast, he got up. Then falling prostrate on
the floor, he wept bitterly over his past disorders,
implored pardon of God and made a firm resolution of amendment. Dressing himself in great
haste, he hurried off to the Saint, who was waiting
for him and who was assured by light from on
high of his conversion. He made his Confession
and from then on practiced the holiness and regu-
larity of life befitting his calling.[1]

The Saint was on another occasion preaching
at Pampeluna when he was suddenly enraptured
in the midst of his discourse. Returning to himself, he informed his audience that God commanded him to interrupt his preaching in order to
put a stop to a grievous offense that was being
committed in the city. He immediately descended
from the pulpit and, followed by a group of persons surprised and curious to see what would
happen, directed his steps toward a sumptuous
palace. The doors were closed. He touched one of

them with his hand, and it immediately opened of itself. When he entered, he declaimed with great energy against the impure vice while traversing the halls and chambers. They who followed him saw no one, but they distinctly heard the voices of the wretched people who were the victims of their sinful passion. St. Vincent implored them to desist, but they persisted in their sin. He threatened them with terrible chastisements, but they derided him all the more. Then God avenged Himself on their crime—they were changed into statues of marble. The Saint entered the chamber and disclosed to the bystanders the terrible way in which Divine Vengeance had chastised the crimes and obstinacy of those unhappy people. Nevertheless, being touched with compassion, he approached the statues and, breathing into their mouths, restored them to life. This act of charity also changed their hearts of stone into hearts of flesh. They acknowledged their guilt and made their Confession one after the other. Hardly had they received sacramental absolution, than the vehemence of their contrition brought death a second time, for they expired at the feet of the Saint. God blessed the zeal of His servant by this wonderful conversion to show how agreeable to Him was his charity, which never shrank from any means calculated to save the souls of his neighbors.[2]

So great was St. Vincent's love for souls that he unhesitatingly accepted the most heroic sacrifices to insure their salvation. When preaching in Spain, he was one day called to a dying person older in sin than in years. The latter was unwilling to be spoken to on the subject of Confession and was resolved to crown the wickedness of his life with final despair. Vincent arrived, but all his advances were met by a steady refusal on the part of the sick man. Then the Saint said to him, "I assure you that God has pardoned you. I have prayed for you and have obtained mercy; nay, more: whatever merits I may have, these I have entirely made over to you." At these words, which marked such singular generosity, the troubled soul of the dying man was somewhat reassured, and he replied, "I will make my Confession, but you must beforehand put in writing both the petition for pardon and the promised donation." "With all my heart," said the Saint, and he immediately wrote with his own hand on a sheet of paper a prayer to the God of mercy on behalf of that poor repentant sinner, and at the same time supplicated the Divine Bounty to transfer to him all the merits which he himself might have acquired throughout the course of his life. He confessed the dying man, then he placed in his hands the written document. The latter soon after entered into a sweet agony and peacefully expired. Scarcely had he drawn his last breath than the document disappeared. It followed the soul to the tribunal of the Supreme Judge. The Divine Majesty was pleased to give it a public and authentic testimony, in order that the fact, coming to the knowledge of sinners, might inspire them also with obedience to the word of His ambassador. While Vincent was preaching in a public square to more than thirty thousand persons, they beheld the sheet of paper which he had given to the dying person descend from Heaven, and it fell into his hands. This was an object of general astonishment, for no one was cognizant of the mystery. But their surprise knew no bounds when Vincent, having read the document, told the people that it was the petition written with his own hand, given to the sick man who had scandalized the city by his sinful conduct and who had resolved to die impenitent. The Saint told them that that man had heard him, that he himself had confessed him, that when dying he had taken that piece of paper and presented it at the tribunal of God, that the Sovereign Judge had accepted it, that he had signed its authenticity, and finally, that he had a perfect certainty of that soul's salvation.[3] We can easily judge the impression which this surprising miracle would produce on the minds of the multitude. As for ourselves, what excites our admiration even more is the charity of the Saint, who so completely forgot himself that he could only think of others, and who joyfully relinquished all the spiritual treasures of his life, that he might insure the eternal felicity of his neighbor. How could sinners after this resist such sincere proofs of love and devotedness? We need not therefore be surprised at the extraordinary success of St. Vincent Ferrer. If faith removes mountains, we must not forget that love is as strong as death, and that nothing can resist it. (*Cant.* 8).

The Saint, formed in the school of Blessed Dominic, possessed in the highest degree every moral virtue: justice, obedience, temperance, chastity, poverty, mortification, humility, sweetness, affability, generosity, magnanimity, courage and constancy. Many examples of these are to be found.

First of all, let us not pass over in silence the following example which shows the perfection of his chastity: He was already a religious when certain envious persons, annoyed at the praises that were passed on his virtue and urged on by diabolical inspiration, bribed with a large sum of money a profligate woman to secrete herself in the Saint's cell. They helped her to accomplish her purpose one winter evening while he prolonged his prayer in the Church. When Vincent opened the door and found the miserable creature seated at the foot of his bed, he thought at first it was an artifice of the devil, who wished to tempt him under that seducing form. He made the Sign of the Cross and exclaimed: "What doest thou here, Satan, enemy of God?" "I am not Satan," answered the profligate, "but a young woman who can no longer resist the love she bears toward you." She was about to continue, but the Saint interrupted her in a brief and imperious tone: "Go from here, wretch," cried he, "and be careful lest a sudden death overtake you by reason of your frightful iniquity! How dare you attempt to sully my body and soul, which from my childhood I have consecrated to Jesus Christ?" Whether from fright or from excessive impudence, the unhappy woman remained immovable. Then Vincent cast some burning cinders from a brazier on the floor, and kneeling upon them, he said: "Come if you dare. Come and cast yourself on this fire; it is not so terrible as that of Hell." At this spectacle, the woman became half-dead, weeping, sobbing, imploring pardon of the Saint and promising him that she would entirely change her life. She disclosed to him the names of those who had led her to this act. Vincent dismissed her, commanding her to conceal the names of her accomplices. But she did not promise silence. On the following morning, she related all and covered with shame those who sought to calumniate and dishonor the Saint. The sinner became sincerely converted.[4]

Despite his passionate and ardent character,

Vincent Ferrer exhibited a patience that was proof against every trial. From his childhood he strove to repress anger. One day, a servant in his father's house blasphemed the Name of Our Lord. Vincent, following the first impulse of his indignation, severely reprimanded him. The latter did not profit by it; he replied with injurious epithets and even struck the child. The young Saint, instead of crying and complaining, changed his zeal to meekness and said to the man: "Dear brother, I owe you much; in chastening me you have taught me the prudence which it is proper to observe in correcting persons older than oneself, and especially servants who are in anger. I shall know it another time." The man, whose name was Alexis Raffet, was so astonished at this patience, this heroic sweetness and humility, that he cast himself at the child's feet to ask his pardon and implored him not to mention to his father or mother what had happened. Vincent threw himself into his arms, and with a radiant countenance, said to him, "Do not fear; they shall know nothing of what has passed. Only, my Dear Friend, do not blaspheme in the future."[5]

When afflicted with great suffering toward the end of his life, he underwent a surgical operation without uttering the slightest groan. He only invoked tenderly the sweet names of Jesus, Mary or some Saint. He drank without exterior repugnance the bitter draughts that were administered to him. He was frequently during the course of his apostolate almost stifled by the people, and once he remained as dead under the feet of the multitude. He made no complaint, and on rising, exhibited a placid countenance, as though he had suffered nothing. When his infirmities obliged him to the use of an ass, he from time to time sustained severe falls, yet on these occasions he never exhibited the least sign of impatience. But, as his disciples remarked with astonishment, in reward of this virtue, God never permitted him to suffer any inconvenience from these accidents. Not only did Vincent practice this virtue, which renders a man amiable to those who live with him, but he also inculcated it in others with great tact. One day a woman came to him complaining bitterly of the bad treatment she had to endure from her husband. "Teach me, my good Father," said she, "an efficacious method of preserving peace at home, in order that my husband may cease to ill-use me both by word and deed." The Saint allowed her uninterrupted speech, well knowing the cause of the evil for which she sought a remedy; it was only her talkativeness and petulance; she irritated her husband by her chattering and provoking answers. Then the Saint quietly said to her: "If you wish to put an end to these disagreeable scenes, go to the Brother Porter of our convent and bid him give you a jug of water from the well which is in the middle of the cloister. When your husband returns home, take at once a mouthful of this water without swallowing it and retain it for a considerable time in your mouth. If you do this, I assure you that your husband will no more be angry with you and will become as meek as a lamb." The woman immediately hastened to execute the Saint's advice, seeing that the remedy was by no means a difficult one. When the husband returned home and began to show symptoms of irritation, she ran to the jug and filled her mouth with water, which she retained as long as she was able, the result being that, meeting with no reply, the husband himself was silent. He wondered at this, but said nothing, and thanked God for having changed the heart and closed the mouth from which proceeded all their disputes. Having put this advice into practice many times, and always with the same success, the woman returned to St. Vincent overflowing with thanks to him for having taught her so excellent a remedy. Then the Saint, speaking to her with sweetness, plainly told her: "The remedy which I have taught you, my daughter, is not the water from the well, as you suppose, but silence. By holding your tongue, you have preserved peace between yourself and your husband. He had scarcely entered the house, when you irritated him by your troublesome questions; it was your own fault if this anger increased; your provoking rejoinders were the cause of it. Be silent in the future, and you will always live in peace with your husband." Hence the common proverb in Valencia when a woman complained of her husband; she was answered: "Fill your mouth with water, and what St. Vincent said will come to pass."[6]

—SECTION FIVE—
THE MARVELOUS GIFTS WHICH SHONE FORTH IN ST. VINCENT FERRER.

Chapter 13

St. Vincent Ferrer Favored with a Multitude of
Visions, Revelations and Ecstasies—The Secrets
Of Hearts Revealed to the Saint.

VINCENT Ferrer daily beheld in his private
prayers, and even in the course of his apostolic preaching, either pious souls who still lived
on earth, or the souls in Purgatory, or the Saints in
Paradise, the Angels, the Blessed Virgin Mother of
God and Our Lord Himself.

He was praying one day for the conversion of
souls when he beheld a fervent nun of the Order of
St. Francis doing as he did; her eyes were bathed
in tears, and she was prostrate at the feet of Our
Lord. He heard Christ say to her: "Thy tears, My
daughter, are most agreeable, and I joyfully hear
thy prayers; but these ungrateful and guilty people
who outrage the law and blaspheme My Name
have little claim on My pity; on the contrary, they
provoke My justice." At the same time Our Lord
revealed to the Saint that this nun was Colette, the
illustrious Saint who labored with much fruit for
the reformation of the Sisters of her Order. Vin-

cent was filled with admiration and delight at this spectacle.

On another day, while he celebrated Mass at Valencia, on his return from one of his apostolic journeys, he saw appear before him, and as it were over the altar, a woman surrounded with flames and holding in her arms a little disfigured child. Astonished at such a vision, he adjured the woman, in the Name of the Lord, to tell him who she was and what she wanted. She was one of his own sisters, named Frances, who had been dead some time. She had married a rich merchant. The latter having been obliged to undertake a long journey, the chief servant of his house profited by his absence to constrain the merchant's wife to commit sin with him, under the threat of death unless she consented. She was weak enough to yield; but recovering from her fright, and being covered with shame in her own eyes, she poisoned the man to rid herself of his foul presence; and as she had conceived, she destroyed the offspring before it was born. To complete her misery, she dared not avow these crimes in Confession and so she added to these murders numerous sacrileges. At length, remorse filled her soul. She made her Confession to an unknown priest, with the greatest sorrow for her crimes, and died three days afterward. God having condemned her to an expiation of terrible duration [in

Purgatory], she addressed herself to her brother to abridge its length. She indeed appeared again to St. Vincent three days afterward in glory, crowned with flowers, surrounded by Angels and ascending to Heaven; thus did she disappear from his sight.[1] The rest of his family gave him the purest consolations. He beheld the souls of his father, mother, brother and other sisters ascend to Heaven without passing through the flames of Purgatory.

While he was one night sleeping in the Convent at Cervera in Spain, St. Dominic appeared, and the rays of light which surrounded him were so bright that they woke Vincent. "My son," said the glorious Father, "the Lord has commanded me to visit you to impart to you most useful instructions which will redouble your ardor and enable you to pursue the course of your apostolic preaching with much fruit. Yes, my son," added the Founder of the Order, "persevere till death in the path on which you have entered. Your works are most pleasing to God. The fidelity with which you discharge the duties of your profession shall merit for you in Heaven the same degree of glory which I myself enjoy. You resemble me perfectly in the observance of the rule and in your personal holiness, virginal purity and zeal for the salvation of souls; like me, you have been sent by Christ to preach and to teach the Gospel truth; only I am the root and trunk of the Order; you are one of the most fruitful branches and fairest flowers engrafted thereon. Persevere then in your way, so that having arrived at the term of your pilgrimage, you may reign eternally with me among the happy citizens of Heaven."

Vincent humbled himself profoundly, thanked the blessed Father for his precious visit and fervently commended himself to his intercession. While this interview lasted, the two Saints spoke so loudly that several of Vincent's companions, who slept in an adjoining room, were awakened. Peter de Moya, peeping through the chinks of the door, saw in Vincent's cell a venerable religious, whose countenance was so radiant with light that the whole place was illumined. On the following morning, his disciples, conjecturing that their spiritual master had received some extraordinary heavenly favor, asked him what religious had appeared to him on the previous night. Vincent was desirous of concealing from them the favor he had received, but they importuned him so much that he related to them what had occurred, requesting them to preserve a rigorous silence on the subject of the vision till his death.[2]

One of the most interesting angelical manifestations occurring to our Saint was that of the Guardian Angel of Barcelona. On entering the city, he saw near the gate a young man resplendent with light, holding a sword in one hand and a shield in the other. The Saint asked him what he was doing with arms in that place. "I am the Guardian Angel of Barcelona," he said; "this city is under my protection." In the first sermon which followed this remarkable vision, Vincent related what had happened to him, congratulated the inhabitants of Barcelona on their happiness and exhorted them to offer their thanksgiving to the Angel who guarded them. This they did by building a small chapel on the very spot where the Angel appeared to the holy preacher.

Very frequently also, when Vincent was in the pulpit, the people saw the Angels forming a crown around his head.[3]

One cannot doubt that the visions of the Blessed Mother of God to her faithful servant Vincent were also very frequent. A sacred image of Mary was for a long time preserved in the convent at Valencia, which it is said spoke to him. And St. Louis Bertrand being one day asked if this were true, he gave this remarkable answer: "It spoke not merely twice or three times, but continually, for Mary dealt with Vincent as the tenderest of mothers."[4]

It is clear also that Our Lord Jesus Christ frequently appeared to him, as at Avignon and Perpignan, when He Himself miraculously cured him. But Vincent's humility concealed those graces so effectually that they seldom came to the knowledge of men. It was by pious stratagem only that he was seen raised in the air in his cell and surrounded in the night with an immense light. While he was staying in a Benedictine priory at Josselin in Brittany, the monks frequently went in the night to watch him in his cell through the chinks in the door; they beheld him sleeping on the floor, with his Bible for a pillow, and his face beaming with a splendor which illumined the cell. Amazed at this spectacle, the good monks permitted the Count de Rohan to witness it, on whose mind it made such a deep impression that he from that moment became an example of sincere piety.[5] The Saint received these choice graces with deep humility and a wise caution. He counseled his disciples not curiously to desire them, and wisely to resist them, seeing that the spirit of darkness, transforming himself into an angel of light, may easily substitute himself for God in these circumstances, when they were not animated with the requisite dispositions.

The discernment of spirits was marvelous in the Saint. There was at Barcelona a person named Louis Cataldo, who suffered severe pains in the head. This man had no faith in the daily miracles of Vincent, but experiencing no relief from any remedy, he went one day in desperation to the church of the Friar Preachers, and at the moment when Vincent descended from the pulpit, he said to him: "Father, for two years I have suffered frightful pains in the head; I implore you to cure me." The Saint replied: "I am neither God nor a doctor to cure you." At this answer, the sufferer understood that the Saint knew the secret thoughts of his incredulous heart. But aided by God's grace and putting aside all hesitation, he said to him once more: "And yet I firmly hope you will grant me this favor." "But do you really believe it?" said the Saint. "Certainly, my Father," answered the other. Then Vincent placed his hand on Louis's head, saying, "Thou art already cured; thank God, and believe that they who serve Him are invested with great power." The cure was so complete that, during the space of the forty additional years which he lived, the man never experienced the slightest pain in the head.

One day, a person named Gaja came to the Saint and importuned him to admit him into his company. Vincent was very willing to receive him, but told him to sell beforehand all that he possessed and distribute the price of it to the poor. This man obtained 400 gold pieces by his sale. He secretly kept back 200 of them, gave the rest to the poor and then went to inform the Saint that he had executed his commands. At these words, Vincent, fixing his eyes on him, said: "Man of little faith, thinkest thou that the least thing would be wanting to thee in my company? Thou imaginest, perhaps, that I am ignorant of what thou hast done? Go, thou hast given only half of thy money to the poor. I refuse thee as a member of my company; I want no disciples of this stamp." At this reproof, so unlooked for, the man cast himself at the Saint's feet, implored his forgiveness and promised to bestow on the poor the sum which he had withheld. This promise satisfied Vincent, who seeing him resolved to obey, tenderly embraced him and admitted him into his company.

One of the pilgrims who followed the Apostle of God was interiorly disposed to doubt the miracles and conversions which he saw accomplished by the Thaumaturgus. He watched his words and actions in order to turn them to ridicule, after the manner of the Pharisees, whose eyes were always fixed on the Saviour of men with a view to finding fault. One day Vincent accosted him and looking intently at him, began to lay open to him all the thoughts of his heart, all the censures and criticisms which weighed upon his soul in regard to his apostolic doings. He did it so truthfully and with such energy that the disciple, confused and repentant, threw himself on his knees and humbly besought his pardon. Vincent readily accorded it to him, but at the same time gave him a paternal caution. "Pay attention," said he, "to what you do yourself, and not to what others do."

An Aragonian named Don Ferdinand belonged also to the Saint's company. He was not sincere; he affected exteriorly a sanctity which he had not at heart, and was all the more culpable, inasmuch as he removed himself further from the true perfection taught by the holy master and generally practiced by his companions. This hypocrisy was so exquisitely refined, so artfully concealed from the eyes of all that, humanly speaking, it was impossible to detect it. But celestial light never failed St. Vincent in penetrating a secret. He once took the person aside and said to him: "Really, if I did not know you would one day undertake great hardships for my honor, I would chase you from my company, for you are wicked." These words covered Don Ferdinand with confusion and filled him with remorse. "Dear master," answered he, "pray to God for me." The Saint replied: "I have already done so, and it has been granted that you shall not be condemned. You shall, moreover, prosper exceedingly on the earth and live for many years. Procure then the book entitled, *Du Mépris du Monde*[6] and read it." It turned out as St. Vincent predicted. Don Ferdinand, in fact, embraced a most virtuous life; he prospered in his career and even became chaplain to the King and Bishop of Telesia. In the year 1454 he was at Naples, where he contributed to the canonization of St. Vincent by rendering testimony to many miracles which he had seen performed with his own eyes. He left behind him so high an opinion of his virtues as to verify the latter part of his master's prophecy: "You shall not be condemned."

When he heard the Confessions of sinners, Vincent miraculously assisted them in discovering the faults which escaped their recollection. But, what is still more remarkable is that, during his sermons, he would sometimes fix his eyes upon people whom he had never before seen or heard; then he would enter on the subject of the sins which they usually committed, laying open the circumstances so clearly and with such precision that the people were accustomed to say: "This man is truly a Saint, for he knows the most hidden secrets of our hearts." Whether it was a usurer, an adulterer, a thief, an assassin, a person guilty of the foulest crimes, the Saint's words came home to him with such truthful effect that at the end of the discourse he succeeded, by his close reasoning and an eloquence inflamed with love, in converting him from vice to a life of justice and penance.

God exhibited to the prophet Ezechiel the abominations of His people at the time wherein that prophet lived, that he might exhort them to repentance. He bestowed the same lights on Vincent Ferrer. Wherever he preached, he saw the sins of people and the wounds of souls; it was this that rendered his speech so full of wisdom, so prudent and efficacious in correcting vice.[7]

Chapter 14

St. Vincent Ferrer Endowed with the Gift of Prophecy—The Grace of Miracles Accorded, without Measure, to the Saint.

GOD, of Himself, and through the instrumentality of His Saints, revealed to Vincent Ferrer his own predestination and the glory which would surround his name in the Catholic Church. This was not enough: He moreover willed that the Saint's own lips should announce it to the people. One one occasion, therefore, when preaching at Alexandria in Piedmont, he thus spoke to his listeners: "My brethren, I have good news to tell you: There is a young man among you who will be the glory of the Seraphic Order [the Franciscans] and of Italy [he signified St. Bernardine of Siena]. He will take my place among you when I shall have returned to Spain. His heavenly life and holy teaching will bear most abundant fruits; he will become a great light in the Church, which will honor him before it accords the same honor to myself." The prophecies contained in these words were literally fulfilled. Bernardine of Siena, having entered the Order of St. Francis, preached in Italy, died in 1444 and was canonized in 1450, some years before Vincent was himself canonized.

Preaching one day at Valencia, the Saint openly declared that he should die in the odor of sanctity in a country far away from his native land, and that his body would perform a great number of miracles. The prophetic spirit unfolded itself still further in him; he even specified many of the particular circumstances of his canonization and especially the personage who would render him that honor.

This occurred many times. The first was at the Chateau de Canals, not far from the town of Xativa. On passing the Chateau, he met a lady named Francina, the wife of Dominic Borgia. She was a little advanced in pregnancy, but was not certain of it. Vincent assured her of this and added: "The child which you bear will one day be Pope." Some time afterwards, in the year 1378, say the historians, passing by the same place on his way to preach at Xativa, Vincent saw Francina holding in her arms a child which she had given birth to only a few days before. "Take great care of this little child," said he; "it will be Pope and will canonize me." Some months elapsed, and one day when Vincent was in the company of some of the child's relations, it chanced that his mother arrived with him in her arms. The Saint embraced him;

then turning to the company, he said, "Kiss the feet of this child; a time will come when he will be created Pope and when he will canonize me." When the child was three years old, one of his uncles again presented him to the holy religious, who said, "Make him study well; let him go to school, for he will one day become Pope and will render great honors to me." Toward the year 1400, when preaching at Lerida, Vincent had among his listeners this young man whose infancy he had blessed, and of whom he had predicted so glorious a future. The student was so much impressed by the preacher that he went to see him after the sermon and said to him, "You preach marvelously well, my Father; you will be a Saint!" "And it will be you who will canonize me," replied Vincent. This prophecy, so often repeated, was fully realized. Alphonsus Borgia became a learned theologian and a distinguished canonist; he was Canon of Lerida and Barcelona, curé of the parish of St. Nicholas, Bishop of Valencia, and at last Cardinal. When he had been elevated to so high a dignity, he felt so certain, on the Saint's assurance, of being one day elected Pope, that he made a vow to pursue the Turks from the moment he became Sovereign Pontiff. In 1455 he proclaimed the sanctity of him who had so often announced his own glorious destiny.

To enumerate the Saint's prophecies would be

impossible. They had reference to individuals, communities, cities, kingdoms and the Universal Church.

Peter de Luna, abandoned by everyone, still obstinately persisted in his claims. "His ambition will be punished," said Vincent Ferrer; "this man will sink into universal contempt, and his body will become the plaything of children." This latter circumstance was verified at the time of the wars of succession in Spain at the beginning of the eighteenth century. The French being in possession of the Isle of Peniscola, some children dug open the tomb of that obstinate man and took out of it the bones, which served them as playthings for several days.

Vincent gave at the Convent of the Friar Preachers at Valencia some interesting sermons on the Saints who would flourish therein. This convent was truly a nursery of Saints. We may cite, among others, the Blessed Dominic of Mont-Majeur, Amateur Espy, John Micon and especially the illustrious St. Louis Bertrand, with a great number of his disciples.

We have spoken of the prophecy which the Saint uttered at Barcelona, when the city was made desolate by a terrible famine. He announced in the city of Teulada, which was often ravaged by the Moors, that it should be henceforth under cover of their incursions, and he added that the plague should never touch them. Both of these prophecies were marvelously fulfilled.

Vincent loved his country. He foretold with tears the revolutions which would disturb it. When they burst forth, he made every effort to restore peace to the State, and by his prayers, prudence and firmness, he succeeded therein. He foretold, moreover, the decisive expulsion of the Moors from Spain. In less than a century later, Granada, their last bulwark, fell into the hands of Isabella the Catholic.

But according to the Venerable Seraphin de la Porretta, a most learned and holy religious of our Order, the distinctive characteristic of Vincent Ferrer was the preaching and announcing of the Last Judgment. Yes, Vincent was the Angel of the Apocalypse, as he proved at Salamanca by raising a woman to life. He proclaimed that awful day as imminent and near. Let us observe, however, that this prophecy was comminatory [i.e., a threat], as was that of Jonas at Nineve. Had not the world been converted by the preaching of our Saint, it would not have subsisted to the present hour. But it changed, as did the Ninevites, and like Nineve it was saved, and its existence thus prolonged. God has delayed the execution of that terrible sentence, according to the expression of St. Ambrose, founded on Holy Scripture: "God will know how to change His resolution, provided you amend your life." Otherwise, considering the rapidity with which time flows by, one might well believe in the proximity of the End of the World and of the Judgment which will follow.

St. Vincent foretold that a society of apostolic men would rise up in the latter times, who would be eminent for their piety and whose zeal would be extraordinary. We flatter ourselves that this prophecy is being realized in the Order of St. Dominic itself, as has been shown in another work.[1] An author writes: "The life of St. Vincent Ferrer was a standing miracle whose object was the living, the dead, persons in health, those who were sick, the earth, the air and the sea—in a word, all the elements."[2] But what appears to us even more remarkable is the facility with which the holy Thaumaturgus wrought those wonders. It was as easy for him to do this, says the Venerable Louis de Granada, as it is for us to lift the hand to the mouth. It was an habitual gift of his, a gift which he possessed even before his birth, as we have shown at the beginning of this work—a gift which accompanied his childhood, which increased with his youth and attained perfection in his manhood, especially when commissioned by Our Lord to evangelize the world during the latter twenty years of his life. It was during that period that he regularly performed them every morning after his preaching: *"Ring the bell of miracles,"*[3] he was accustomed to say to one of his disciples.

He was sometimes interiorly inspired not to cure all who presented themselves; but when they returned at the appointed hour, he always finished by restoring them to health. Had he in the course of those years performed but eight miracles a day, they would have reached the extraordinary number of fifty-eight thousand four hundred. But this calculation clearly falls far short of the mark, since it is a well-attested fact that the Saint wrought them not only in public assemblies, and in the pulpit, but even while traveling, while resting on his journeys—at every moment, so to speak. Hence the common saying among his biographers: "It was a miracle when he did not work miracles, and the greatest miracle was when he performed none at all." St. Louis Bertrand confirms their testimony: "God," says this Saint, "sanctioned the teaching of Vincent Ferrer by so many miracles, that there never was a Saint since the days of the Apostles to our own time who wrought more. God alone knows their number, as He alone knows the number of the stars that people the firmament."[4] We have already related many of these miracles and shall record others in the Third Part of our work; still, we will relate here some which deserve to be known and remembered.

On the Feast of Saints Peter and Paul one year

[June 29], a frightful storm burst over the city of Barbastro in Catalonia at the moment when the Saint was unvesting after Mass. The rain fell in torrents, the lightning flashed and thunder rolled with such terrific effect as to threaten all around with instant destruction. The Saint, leaving the church, made the Sign of the Cross with holy water, at which the storm was immediately appeased, and the sky became serene. Ascending the pulpit, he exhorted the people to return thanks to the holy Apostles for the favor they had just received and said that, unless they had interceded with God, there would have remained neither leaves on the trees nor green herbs in the country. He added: "Unless you beseech God to preserve your goods and promise to make a holy use of them, next year another tempest will devastate the entire land." Eleven months later, a terrible storm literally accomplished this prediction.[5]

At Berga in Catalonia, St. Vincent was one day preaching with great fervor and unction on the most Holy Name of Jesus. A violent rain, which had been expected for many hours, at length fell with great impetuosity. His audience hastily dispersed to find shelter. Some fled to the house of a Moorish smith and sought refuge in a workshop built of dry wood. A good woman said to the smith, "Why do you not come, as we do, to hear the sermons of the holy Father?" At these words the Mohammedan became furious. "Cursed be your holy Father!" cried he, and with the sparks from his forge setting fire to the dried wood that was arranged around the workshop, he added, "We shall now see what use you make of those sermons." The fire rapidly spread to the numerous materials that lay about, and the unfortunate people were speedily surrounded with flames. In their danger, they invoked the Holy Name of Jesus. "O sweet Jesus," said they, "your preacher, Master Vincent, told us that your Name is the help of Christians; deliver us from this pressing danger!" In an instant the flames were extinguished, and the wood even ceased to smoke. This miracle astonished the Mohammedan. He was converted, and three days later St. Vincent baptized him.[6]

On another occasion, the Saint with all his company crossed the Ebro to Tortosa in boats that were too small to contain, without danger, the number of persons who filled them. The water soon got into the boats, and they were on the point of sinking. Cries of distress were heard on every side. They implored the Saint to save them. He made the Sign of the Cross on the river, and in an instant, the boats ceased to take in water and reached the shore in safety.

Often St. Vincent miraculously multiplied bread and wine and other foodstuffs.

Wonderful, indeed, were the ways in which he

manifested his gifts. Well-attested documents show that multitudes of people witnessed him, in the middle of his discourse, suddenly assume wings and fly off to console and encourage some suffering person who sought his help; and having performed that act of charity, he would return in the same manner to continue his preaching. It is on this account that, like the Angels, St. Vincent is represented with wings.[7]

God accorded the Saint the gift of languages. Into whatever country he entered, although he preached in the Valencian dialect, he was perfectly heard and understood; and in conversation, he spoke in French, Italian, English and German, according to the country he was in, with the ease and fluency of his mother tongue.[8]

St. Vincent exercised a wonderful power over the devils. His word caused them to fly from the bodies of the possessed. It was frequently sufficient for him to touch those who labored under their dominion, in order to deliver them; even his very presence constrained them to depart. But what is still more remarkable is that, in order to put the evil spirits to flight, it was enough to lead those who were possessed to the different places where the Saint was in his journeys; and in places where he was not, they had only to pronounce his name in order to obtain the same result.

It is useful to dwell on the Saint's power in

regard to physical maladies and bodily infirmities. He wrought miraculous cures by the thousands. His power was so supreme in this respect, that he communicated it to others, and even to inanimate objects which he had used. Frequently when people came to ask these sorts of favors of him, he would turn to one of his companions and say: "I have wrought sufficient miracles today and I am tired. Do yourself what is asked of me; the Lord who works through me, will also work through you."

The Prior of the Convent of Lerida one day invited him to visit a lady who was a great benefactress to the Order and who was grievously ill. "My Father," said the Saint, "you ask me to go and see this person that I may cure her by a miracle; why do you not do it yourself? Go, I give you my power, not only for this infirm person, but also for all whom you may meet on the way." The Prior went to see the invalid, and on his way he came across five individuals who were suffering from various wounds. He cured them; then going to the dwelling of the benefactress, he restored her to perfect health in the name of St. Vincent. By the divine favor, he imparted the power of working miracles to another Prior of his Order, throughout his whole life. As with St. Paul, so now with St. Vincent, God communicated the gift of healing even to articles of his dress. One of these was given to a poor but pious woman. The placing of this relic on the heads of the sick cured them, and their alms enabled her to live in comfort.[9]

The Saint resuscitated more than thirty persons during his lifetime. Two of these marvelous resurrections are related in the *Spiritual Instructions* for the fourth and fifth Friday before his Feast. We might relate others as extraordinary, but we must confine ourselves within reasonable limits.

—SECTION SIX—

DEATH OF ST. VINCENT FERRER (1419).

Chapter 15

The Saint Dies at Vannes in Brittany—His
Burial—Canonization—His Relics.

———

DURING a period of sixty-nine years, the
great Apostle of the fifteenth century fought
the painful battle of life. For fifty years he bore the
austere yoke of the religious life; and in the course
of twenty years he traveled throughout Europe,
proclaiming, like another St. Paul, Christ's Kingdom on earth and producing in the souls of men a
salutary change—a holy and happy revolution. It
was but just, then, that the athlete should be recompensed, that the warrior should rest, that the
conqueror should receive the palm of victory.
Brittany was the land chosen, and Vannes was the
city predestined to receive the last breath of the
man of God and to preserve his mortal remains.

When St. Vincent became seriously ill, his disciples, seeing his strength rapidly decline day by
day, earnestly besought him to return to his own
country. They were in hopes that the climate of
Valencia would be favorable to him, and moreover, they were deeply interested in securing for

his own country the possession of his relics. St. Vincent was unwilling to pain the companions of his labors by opposing their wishes. Toward the end of March in the year 1419, taking leave of the Duke of Brittany and the consuls of the city, he quitted Vannes in the night in order to avoid popular excitement. But God's designs were clearly manifested to the Saint and his companions. It was revealed to him that he should die in the city that he was leaving, and on the following morning the company, after a night's journey, were astonished to find themselves at daybreak at the gates of Vannes. The Saint, turning to his companions, said: "My brethren, let us not speak of returning into Spain; you clearly see that it is God's will that I should end my days here." They answered him only with tears. Then, entering by the gate out of which they had passed the night before, he exclaimed: *Haec requies mea in saeculum saeculi*—"this is my rest forever and ever." (*Psalm* 131:14). The people were not slow in discovering who it was that had passed into the city; they ran to meet the Apostle whom they expected never more to behold, while the bells joyfully proclaimed his welcome return. The Duchess of Brittany met him and conducted him to the house of a gentleman named Preulin in order that he might be more conveniently lodged than with Robin Scarb. The Saint would not listen to the proposal.

Instead of exhorting the people to repentance, as he was accustomed to do, he merely told them that he should soon die and commended himself to the prayers of all. This announcement plunged the city into desolation and sorrow, and the multitudes hastened to pour forth their supplications to God that He would prolong the days of His servant.

The holy Apostle was meanwhile ordered to lie down on a bed—he who, until then, had never slept otherwise than on bare boards or on the broken branches of trees. He humbly obeyed. A consuming fever, accompanied with violent pains, soon tormented him. He suffered in every member of his body and seemed on the point of breathing his last. The physicians omitted nothing to save so precious a life, but St. Vincent declared all their remedies useless. He refused everything that could relieve his suffering condition, and it was only at the repeated solicitations of his friends that he could be induced to lay aside a hair shirt which he had worn for many years.

The Saint was joyous amidst his sufferings. His cheerfulness of heart was painted on his tranquil and serene countenance. Pain never troubled this heavenly peace, nor was he ever heard to complain or to show the least sign of impatience. On the contrary, he esteemed himself most happy to resemble his sweet Saviour crucified. He consoled his disciples, who wept around his bed of pain, and exhorted them for the last time to charity, union, simplicity of heart, penance, Christian mortification, zeal for spiritual progress and perseverance. He also told them that he would pray for them.

Ten days before his death, the Bishop of Vannes and the consuls of the city came to ask for his blessing. He received them courteously and with a smiling countenance. This was the 25th of March. He then blessed them and promised them his protection in Heaven. From that time on, he devoted himself to silence, recollection and prayer. He made frequent acts of contrition, as though he had been a great sinner. On Monday in Passion week he received the last Sacraments and the plenary indulgence for the hour of death. Having received the Holy Viaticum, he desired to be left alone for some hours, that he might entertain himself more freely with his Divine Lord. On Tuesday his sufferings became so intense that he could scarcely speak. They then inquired of him where he desired to be buried. "If there had been a convent of St. Dominic at Vannes," said he, "I should have wished to be buried at the feet of my brethren; but as there is not, I leave the matter entirely in the hands of the Bishop and the Duke of Brittany." The fever increased so much in the course of the night that on the following morning he could not articulate. He made signs to a religious to inspire him with holy thoughts and to read him the Passion of Our Lord while he pressed his crucifix to his breast with greater love than ever. Then followed the recommendation of the departing soul, in which the Saint joined with deep devotion. At the close of that solemn act, his features were suddenly transfigured, his forehead beamed with holy joy, and a divine light shone in his countenance and in his eyes: Paradise was open to his view, and he beheld the King of Glory, the Immaculate Queen of Heaven, Angels clothed with dazzling splendor and his own beloved Patron Saints coming forth to meet him. He joined his hands as in prayer and implanted on his crucifix a parting kiss. Then, raising his eyes to Heaven, he murmured forth these words, *In manus tuas, Domine, commendo spiritum meum*—"Into Thy hands, O Lord, I commend my spirit" (cf. *Psalm* 30:6), and gave up his soul to God. This occurred on Wednesday evening during Passion week, the 5th of April, 1419.

As soon as his soul took its flight to Heaven, his body assumed an appearance so beautiful, so serene and radiant, that it seemed the reflection of eternal glory. His flesh, so long macerated by fasts and disciplines, hair cloth and the fatigues of the Apostolate, became fair and luminous, as though it were living. So far from inspiring the natural horror which a corpse usually does, his smiling face filled those who looked upon it with senti-ments of love and holy envy. What tears were shed over those sacred remains! The whole city was inconsolable at having lost its treasure and came to venerate the Saint's body. They kissed the hands and feet and touched his forehead with pious objects; his praise was on the lips of all.

At the moment when the pure soul of our Saint was leaving his body, the windows of the room in which he expired suddenly opened of themselves, and a flock of small birds were seen to enter. They were not larger than butterflies, very beautiful and whiter than snow. They filled not only the cham-ber, but the whole house. When the Saint drew his last breath, these little birds disappeared, but left the place scented with a delicious perfume. All were of the opinion that these were the Angels, who had come in that form to meet the Saint and conduct his soul in triumph to Paradise.

Another prodigy was witnessed at the same moment. John Liquillic of Dinan had in his pos-session several candles which had been used at the Saint's Mass and which he carefully preserved in a case in his room under lock and key. On the sec-ond of February, 1419, being desirous to light them in honor of the Blessed Virgin, he went to get them, but they were nowhere to be found. All his efforts to discover what had become of them were of no avail. But what was his astonishment

when, on the 5th of April of the same year, he
found all the candles in the case, where they were
miraculously lighted! He called his wife to witness the marvel, but neither of them at that
moment understood its meaning. When it was
afterwards known that that was the very day on
which St. Vincent died, the prodigy was easily
explained.[1]

Grave discussions arose when there was a ques-
tion of deciding who should be privileged to pos-
sess the Saint's precious remains. The religious of
his own Order wished to transport them to the
Convent of Valencia, to which he belonged, or at
least to one of their houses that was nearest to
Vannes, for there was no establishment of the
Order in that city. The Franciscans, on the other
hand, reclaimed against this proceeding, saying
that, as the union of the two Orders of St. Francis
and St. Dominic obliged them to afford mutual
hospitality in all places where one or the other of
them had no monastery of their Order, it devolved
on them to give a place of burial to the Saint, inasmuch as there was no Dominican Convent in
Vannes. But the Bishop—aware of the answer that
St. Vincent, before his death, had given to Father
Ives of Millereu and the Duke of Brittany respecting himself—decreed that the Saint's body should
be buried in the Cathedral. He therefore ordered
that the house in which the sacred remains lay

should be closed and a guard of soldiers set to watch it, and that the burial should take place at the hour of sunset. A solemn procession consisting of the Bishops of Vannes and St. Malo, the secular and regular clergy and the nobility and the people, accompanied the Saint's body to the Cathedral. It was exposed in the center of the choir, the face and hands being uncovered. On the following morning, when the solemn obsequies had been performed, the Bishop of Vannes deposited with his own hands the precious remains in a marble vault, opposite the episcopal throne and near the high altar.

Numerous miracles soon proclaimed the glory of this holy man. In the evening of the day on which the obsequies took place, a leper, prostrating himself on the slab of the Saint's tomb, was suddenly cured. Multitudes of invalids followed his example and returned cured. "Four hundred persons," says Guyard, "recovered their health merely by lying on the bed whereon the Saint died." The sculptor who carved the tomb drew from the Saint's gratitude a marvelous recompense. His leg was dangerously wounded, and no human remedy could heal it although he had tried everything. He at length had recourse to St. Vincent. "Friend of God," said he, "good Father Vincent, pray to God for me!" He had scarcely said these words when the pains in his leg suddenly left him, and in a few days the wound closed, and he was perfectly cured. These favors increased the devotion of the people, and to satisfy it, they constructed an altar over the tomb. Other altars were erected in his honor in several of the Dominican Churches. The process of his canonization soon followed, but various circumstances conspired to delay it. At length, Pope Calixtus III whose elevation to the Supreme Pontificate he had so often foretold—together with the honors which he himself would receive from him—officially proclaimed the sanctity of the servant of God on the 29th of June, 1455, and fixed the celebration of his Feast on the 5th of April, the anniversary of his death. The successor of Calixtus III, Pius II published the Bull of Canonization.

The canonization was celebrated at Vannes with indescribable solemnity. The Saint's body was taken from the tomb wherein it was buried. It was still entire, as on the day of his death. It was placed in front of the altar to be exposed to the veneration of the faithful. Many miracles which were accomplished on that day increased their confidence and devotion. A year afterward, the relics were translated to another tomb more costly than the first and more fitting to contain them. Grand fêtes (feasts or festivals) were celebrated on the occasion, and a considerable number of distinguished personages took part in them.

The inhabitants of Vannes were more than once exposed to the danger of losing St. Vincent's body. Toward the middle of the sixteenth century, a Spanish corps, sent by Philip II, having effectually protected the city against the attacks of the heretics, the Cathedral chapter were desirous of testifying their gratitude to the commander, Don Juan d'Aguilar, and offered him a large fragment of one of the rib bones. But the soldiers had conceived the design to carry off the whole body. Fortunately, the canons were apprised of it in time. During the night they concealed the shrine which contained the relics, and did it so secretly that it remained unknown from the year 1590 until 1637. It was discovered at this date by the Bishop of Vannes. The holy relics were then verified, and a second translation took place on the 6th of September, a day which has been annually observed ever since to commemorate that event.

During the years of revolutionary trouble and disorder which stained the decline of the last century, the people of Vannes were fortunate enough to recover the relics of St. Vincent Ferrer from the hands of the sacrilegious robbers, who profaned the churches and altars to enrich themselves with the sacred spoils. St. Vincent's body was always regarded as a precious treasure in the Cathedral of Vannes. Time has not lessened the devotion of Brittany toward its great Apostle and glorious

Patron. On the first Sunday of September, the Saint's relics are annually carried in procession through the streets of Vannes, escorted by the civil, military and judicial authorities, and followed by an immense crowd of the townspeople. In times of public calamity especially, these venerable relics are borne in solemn procession through the city to reanimate the hope and piety of its people. Only priests have the honor of carrying them. The houses before which they pass are hung with white draperies. During the cholera of 1857, a similar procession took place in Vannes. The city had been desolated by the epidemic, which had until then spared it; and this pious ceremony lessened the intensity of the plague.[2]

Chapter 16

Devotion Offered to St. Vincent Ferrer
by the People and by Holy Personages—
Extraordinary Favors with which the Saint
Rewarded the Devotion of His Clients.

VANNES is not the only place where the veneration of St. Vincent Ferrer flourished. The city which gave birth to the Saint is also distinguished by its devotion to him. In 1460, the inhabitants of Valencia erected in the church of the Friar Preachers a magnificent chapel dedicated to their fellow-countryman, into which in the year 1472 they translated the bones of his father and mother. In accordance with the Saint's prophecy when yet a child, they transformed his house into a sanctuary and placed in it a statue carved in cypress, commemorative of the future destiny which the miraculous child had foretold. This was not accomplished without a miracle. When a search was made in the timber-yards for the trunk of a tree proportioned to the object proposed, none could be found that was large enough. It was at length suggested to take the trunk of a cypress that had been cut down in the garden belonging to the Saint's house. When this piece of timber got into the carver's hands, it miraculously increased to the height and size of an ordinary man.

In 1525, the canons of Vannes bestowed some of the Saint's bones on the Dominicans at Valencia. These relics were received with extraordinary solemnity, on which occasion a young girl, blind from her birth and afflicted with a consuming fever, instantaneously received her sight and recovered her health.

In 1555, the centenary of the Saint's canonization was celebrated in the same city with great pomp and magnificence. In 1565, when a Provincial Council prescribed a liturgical reform, the Archbishop of Valencia wished to reduce the Feast of St. Vincent Ferrer to the rank of an ordinary feast, not of obligation. But the inhabitants of Valencia appealed to the Holy See, and St. Pius V, who then occupied the Pontifical Chair, sanctioned their petition by declaring the Feast of St. Vincent to be of *precept* and confirming the celebration of its octave.

In 1594, Clement VIII ruled that this Feast should be solemnized on the first Monday after the octave of Easter, when the requirements of the rubrics did not admit of its being kept on the 5th of April.

In 1600, Don Juan d'Aguilar, who had obtained

from the canons of Vannes a rib of St. Vincent,
gave it to the Cathedral of Valencia, where it was
received with due reverence and becoming dignity. On this occasion, an infirm woman, who for
nine months had been unable to move without the
aid of crutches, was suddenly cured of her ailment
by recommending herself to the Saint. A person
born mute also received his speech.

The piety of the faithful was not satisfied with
merely keeping St. Vincent's Feast and making it
one of obligation; they celebrated every year,
moreover, with great solemnity the special circumstances of his life. In January, the memory of
his Baptism is honored in the parish of St. Stephen
with all the attendants of religious pomp. On the
5th of February, it was customary to hold a service
in the Saint's cell, which was turned into a chapel
to commemorate the anniversary of his religious
profession. On the 7th of April, he was honored
for the miraculous cure of Dona Blanca, which he
had performed on that day. At the end of June, the
confraternity of the twelve associates of St. Vincent solemnize the anniversary of his canonization. This confraternity was established by
Blessed John Micon. Each of the members was
charged to keep in order for one month the sanc-
tuaries of Valencia dedicated to St. Vincent. In the
episcopal seminary of that city was preserved with
pious care the Saint's doctoral cap, one of his

capuces, the font at which he was baptized, the Bible which he constantly used, with marginal notes in his own handwriting, and one of his cappas with the black capuce. Statues of St. Vincent were multiplied at the corners of the streets and in the public squares. The name of Vincent was commonly given to children. In short, this city spared nothing to glorify the most illustrious of its sons.

Blessed John of Pistoia, a Dominican who was celebrated for his preaching and miracles, spread devotion to our Saint in Tuscany, throughout the rest of Italy and in Dalmatia. It was in consequence of this that, at Prato, between Pistoia and Florence, Blessed Silvester of Marradi, conjointly with Blessed Raphel of Faënza, founded, at the beginning of the sixteenth century, a convent of Sisters of the Third Order under his protection, and it was in this convent that the glorious St. Catherine of Ricci flourished.

Another Religious spread the veneration of the Saint in Sicily. He was from Vannes. When he was fourteen months old, his mother, seized with a fit of madness, cut him in pieces. His father, full of faith in St. Vincent, gathered up the different portions of the body, and carried them to the Saint's tomb. His child was miraculously restored to him, and it was this same child who, out of gratitude, having entered the holy Order of St. Dominic, spent his whole life in propagating devotion to the

Saint who resuscitated him in so marvelous a manner.[1]

Among the holy personages of our Order who have shown particular devotion to the great Apostle of the fifteenth century, we may single out Blessed Catherine Lenzi, Blessed Columba of Rieti, Blessed Lucy of Narni, Blessed Magdalen of Panatieri, Blessed John Micon, Blessed Alexander Capocchi, the holy Pontiff, Blessed Benedict XIII who, on joining the Dominican Order, took the name Vincent: but especially St. Louis Bertrand, the great Thaumaturgus and Apostle of Central America who, like St. Vincent, was a child of Valencia. St. Louis received from his parents the tender devotion toward St. Vincent Ferrer which animated them. When the moment arrived in which he was to decide his vocation, love of solitude drew him to the Chartreux; but his love for St. Vincent was stronger, for it was through love of him that he desired to enter into his Order. Having been appointed Master of Novices, he unceasingly explained to his disciples the Saint's *Treatise on the Spiritual Life*, and profited by the examples it contained to lead them on in the practice of every virtue. "Let us see, my children," he would say at the conclusion of his discourse, "let us see which of us shall be the imitator of this great man, whose equal is not to be found in the world." When he was elected Prior,

St. Louis consulted our Saint, who bid him accept the post and even embraced him by means of one of his statues, at the same time promising him his protection. It is well known with what success St. Louis Bertrand used the prayers of St. Vincent Ferrer in curing the sick.[2]

Outside the Order, we may mention especially Blessed Nicholas Factor, a Franciscan, and the great St. Vincent de Paul, among those who professed a special devotion to the Saint. Blessed Nicholas Factor employed, after the example of St. Louis Bertrand, the prayers of St. Vincent Ferrer in healing the infirm. One day, a Franciscan lay brother, who accompanied him on a visit to the sick, humorously asked him why he, a religious of the Seraphic Patriarch, did not exhort the sick to have recourse to St. Francis and St. Anthony of Padua, rather than to St. Dominic and St. Vincent Ferrer, of another Order. "Hold your tongue, you blockhead," answered the holy man. "In Heaven the saints are not jealous of one another; there we shall all be of one Order, and there will be no distinction of habit. All will be clad in the same garments of glory."

St. Vincent de Paul acknowledged St. Vincent Ferrer as his own special patron. He made his life a daily study and had constantly in his hands the *Treatise on the Spiritual Life*, in order that he might conform thereto not only his own heart and actions, but also those of the priests of his institute.[3]

In his life of St. Vincent Ferrer, the pious Father Teoli devotes numerous pages to the recital of the favors obtained by those who invoked the Saint and who have done honor to him, either in venerating his statues by burning lamps before them or promising to celebrate his novenas and to practice the devotion of the Fridays dedicated to him. We shall record some of the most remarkable of these in order to incite our dear readers to have recourse to this good Father in their spiritual or temporal needs.

Valencia, the cherished city of St. Vincent, never forsook him, and he relieved it in all its necessities. It was he who, by his intercession, procured for it so many holy religious, who, in the course of ages, have labored for the maintenance of the Catholic Faith in its bosom and for the reformation of its morals. He has, moreover, averted from it the visible punishments of divine vengeance, which at times threatened it by reason of its sins.

In the year 1651, Valencia suffered from a dearth of provisions, which affected the entire population. At the moment when the need was most keenly felt, there were at Cagliari, in Sardinia, some grain merchants who were ready to put out to sea with three vessels laden with grain.

While they were debating among themselves concerning the port to which they should sail, they arrived at the Convent of St. Dominic and were accosted by a strange religious of gentle and dignified bearing, who said to them, "I am a native of Valencia, in Spain. I would counsel you to ship your provisions there; you will dispose of them to great advantage, for the inhabitants of that city are at this moment visited with a terrible famine." They promised to follow his advice. On the morning before setting sail, they deemed it expedient to see the religious of that city in order to pay their respects to him and receive his commissions. They inquired of the brother porter, who could give them no information, "For," said he, "we have never seen a religious from Valencia." They then left, but when they had gone a few paces, they perceived in a niche a statue of St. Vincent Ferrer, which perfectly resembled the religious who had spoken to them on the previous evening. Arrived at Valencia on the 17th of January, they failed not to acquaint its inhabitants with what had happened to them. The latter doubted not that the solicitude of their holy Patron had induced him to come to their assistance by appearing to those merchants.

Fifty years afterward, Valencia was subjected to a great drought. Penances and public prayers were offered up, but without any result. There was at that moment an eight-year-old child named Vincent

Villarasa who was suffering from malignant fever and who was on the point of expiring. His father and mother, not having courage to witness the death of their child, retired from the room, leaving him to the care of one of his aunts. But at the moment when the latter thought the child had breathed its last, she suddenly heard him call to her. "Aunt," said the child, "the Saint!" "What do you say?" she asked. He repeated the same words, "Aunt, the Saint!" Hearing this colloquy, the relations and other persons who were in an adjoining room hastened to his bedside and inquired of the child who the Saint was who appeared to him. "It is a saint," answered he, "clothed in black and white; he holds his hands pointing toward Heaven and bears on his head a bright flame." From these words they gathered that he spoke of St. Vincent Ferrer, toward whom the child's father had great devotion. All present knelt down at the side of the bed where the child said the Saint had appeared to him. The father then inquired if the Saint had really spoken. "Yes," said the little Vincent; "he told me that I am already cured and that it will rain tomorrow." This twofold promise was accomplished. On the following morning, the parents conducted their child to the Church of St. Dominic to offer their thanksgiving to St. Vincent, and on that very morning a copious rain fell, which lasted three days and revived the hopes of a good harvest. This fact was authentically attested in a public act. Thus, the inhabitants of Valencia, mindful of the constant protection of their heavenly citizen, have from time immemorial supplicated their esteemed Patron by the following antiphon:

Hic est qui praevaluit amplificare
Civitatem, quique adeptus est gloriam
In conversatione gentis, gloriosus in
Coelis, et Pater noster, Vincentius. Alleluia.

"This is he who prevailed to enlarge the city, and obtained glory in his conversation with the people, and is now clothed with glory in Heaven, our Patron, Vincent. Alleluia."

The religious of the Dominican Convent at Valencia frequently had the consolation of seeing St. Vincent descend from Heaven, join in their holy exercises, accompany them to the refectory, the dormitory and the church. "During the greater part of the night," observed Blessed Dominic Anadon, "we have St. Vincent in the dormitory, on the side of his old cell. We ought," he adds, "to cover that part of the convent with gold and precious stones."[4]

St. Vincent appeared to Blessed Columba of Rieti, who ardently desired to enter the Third Order of St. Dominic, and assuring her that her desires were granted, he exhorted her to prepare herself carefully for it. He also announced to Blessed Magdalen of Panatieri her approaching death, and on leaving her, he left her cell filled with a celestial perfume.

On one occasion, he introduced St. Catherine of Ricci into Heaven—into the presence of Our Lord—and showed her the particular glory which the Saints and Blessed of the Order enjoy. During her agony, the Saint invoked him and obtained through his powerful intercession the gift of final perseverance.[5]

St. Vincent loaded St. Louis Bertrand with his favors. The latter being once grievously ill, was visited by his great friend, Blessed John Ribera, Archbishop of Valencia. In the course of the prelate's visit, a Dominican entered the chamber, and seating himself on the side of the bed, began to console St. Louis with kind words. The sufferer, forgetting the presence of the Archbishop, who was at the other side of the bed, turned his back upon him to listen to the religious. The latter having disappeared some moments afterward, St. Louis, perceiving the fault he had committed, said to the Archbishop: "Do not take amiss, my Lord, at what I did. The religious who conversed with me is St. Vincent Ferrer. I am quite sure of it. He has announced to me the happiest news I could possibly desire—the hour of my passage to Paradise is at hand." At that last moment St. Vincent, with the Son of God and His most holy Mother, assisted him.

St. Louis was one day invited by the same prelate to spend some time in the country. Not being able to go himself, he sent another religious of his Order to take his place, assuring the prelate that the conversation of the latter would be of great spiritual profit to him. The Archbishop, indeed, experienced an extraordinary sweetness in conversing with this religious, and at each of his words the prelate felt the fire of divine love enkindled in his heart in the most lively manner. When the religious departed, he left his host filled with consolation and astonishment; never, not even with St. Louis Bertrand, had he experienced such an abundance of heavenly favors. When the prelate returned to Valencia, his first care was to go to the Convent of St. Dominic to renew the conversation he had with the religious who had been with him in the country. He then asked St. Louis to let him see him again, saying that he had been consoled by him more than he could possibly describe. "I can well believe it, my Lord," said St. Louis, "for that religious was St. Vincent Ferrer, who was pleased to favor your Grace with that visit, in order to recompense and confirm, at the same time, the devotion which you profess toward him."[6]

A nun of the celebrated Convent of Prouille in Southern France, being grievously ill, was miraculously cured by commending herself to St. Vincent Ferrer. We also read in the life of the venerable Mother Agnes of Jesus, a nun of the Convent of St. Dominic of Langeac, that being near death by reason of her age and infirmity, St. Vincent appeared to her, cured her, consoled her and promised her his protection in the design she had formed to enter our holy Order.[7]

Let us then have confidence in this admirable Saint. Let us practice in his honor the various devotions with which piety shall inspire us, and let us invoke him in all our spiritual and temporal needs. This Father, so good and so powerful, will hear us, will grant our petitions and will save us.

"Blessed be God in His
Angels and in His Saints!"

Spread the Faith with . . .

TAN·BOOKS

A Division of Saint Benedict Press, LLC

TAN books are powerful tools for evangelization. They lift the mind to God and change lives. Millions of readers have found in TAN books and booklets an effective way to teach and defend the Faith, soften hearts, and grow in prayer and holiness of life.

Throughout history the faithful have distributed Catholic literature and sacramentals to save souls. St. Francis de Sales passed out his own pamphlets to win back those who had abandoned the Faith. Countless others have distributed the Miraculous Medal to prompt conversions and inspire deeper devotion to God. Our customers use TAN books in that same spirit.

If you have been helped by this or another TAN title, share it with others. Become a TAN Missionary and share our life changing books and booklets with your family, friends and community. We'll help by providing special discounts for books and booklets purchased in quantity for purposes of evangelization. Write or call us for additional details.

TAN Books
Attn: TAN Missionaries Department
P.O. Box 410487
Charlotte, NC 28241

Toll-free (800) 437-5876
missionaries@TANBooks.com